AL SHIELDS

THE WORLD'S FUNNIEST CLOWN SKITS

D1092434

By Barry "Bonzo" DeChant

PICCADILLY BOOKS, LTD
COLORADO SPRINGS, COLORADO

Cover design by Michael Donahue

Piccadilly Books, Ltd.
P.O. Box 25203
Colorado Springs, CO 80936
USA

International sales and inquires contact:
 EPS
 20 Park Drive
 Romford Essex RM1 4LH, UK
or
 EPS
 P.O. Box 1344
 Studio City, CA 91614, USA

Library of Congress Cataloging-in-Publication Date

DeChant, Barry, 1937-
  The world's funniest clown skits / by Barry DeChant.
    p.   cm.
  ISBN 0-941599-31-0 (pbk.)
  1. Clowns. 2. Amateur plays. I. Title.
PN1955.D38 1995   95-10589
791.3'3--dc20   CIP

Simultaneously published in Australia, UK, and USA
Printed in the United States of America

Table of Contents

Foreword

This book belongs in the library of every clown whether beginner or advanced. Mr. DeChant has researched and produced a book of outstanding skits, laid out so that they are easy to understand and simple enough for even the novice clown to perform successfully.

In previewing this book, I realized that I was in the audience when many of these skits were first performed and it brought back great memories of the original performances. Mr. DeChant has graciously recognized the people who wrote and performed the skits whenever possible giving them full credit for their outstanding contributions to clowning.

We are constantly asked where a new clown might obtain a book of good clown skits to perform and teach to others. This book will be highly recommended. A large "thank you" to Mr. DeChant for not letting many of the great skits he has listed be lost in time and ensuring that they will be performed by new generations of clowns.

> —Jack Anderson, past president of:
> Clowns of America, International;
> World Clown Association;
> International Shrine Clown Association

Before You Begin

This book contains 50 tried and tested clown skits. Some have been around for a long time (such as the Balloon Chase originated by the late Otto Griebling), while others have been written recently.

I am responsible for writing and developing some of the skits, while many others have been created and developed by my clown friends and associates.

I encourage you to try to make every performance your best. Your presentation will be successful if you take the time to properly prepare. Pay attention to your appearance. Wear clean, sharp-looking costumes and makeup. A good appearance will help you create the atmosphere for your performance.

All of the skits were designed to be performed by players in clown makeup and costumes. Some characters will require additional pieces of clothing, for example, a doctor will need to wear a white coat, a mindreader may wear a turban and cape. These skits, however, are versatile and can be performed and enjoyed even without traditional clown costumes, as might be the case for a school play or amateur production.

One of the major elements of performing these skits successfully is *practice*. There is no way anyone can perform skits well without a lot of practice. There is no substitute for practice. Rehearsing can be fun as you and your partners work with these skits. Improvise to suit your own tastes and the tastes of your intended audience. Experiment and develop new ways of performing the skits I have outlined. As you make small changes, you will feel more and more like the skits are your own.

Keep in mind that these skits are not "cast in concrete." They do not have to be performed exactly as written in order to be effective. It is more accurate to describe them as being cast in Silly Putty. Have fun with them. Play with them. Use them to entertain others, and don't get so wrapped up in performing the mechanics that you fail to see how your audiences are reacting. Watch your audiences and interact with them. You can even make subtle changes while performing, if your audience has picked up on a specific item you are doing.

Thanks for selecting this book for your library. I wish you great success as you strive to entertain others.

BUSY BEE (One Person)

Number of Clowns: One

Characters: Clown A

Costumes: Regular clown wardrobe

Props: Chair, glass of water

Stage: Chair downstage in center, glass of water on floor behind chair

Setting: In the description that follows, the clown on stage will be referred to as Clown A and the imaginary clown (not on stage) will be referred to as Clown B. This skit is best received by a group that is already familiar with the original, classic Busy Bee skit described on page 45. The skit starts with Clown A entering the stage and looking for his partner. Calls for partner, looks to each side of stage, still calling for the other clown.

The Performance

Clown A: *(Speaks to the audience.)* "Have you seen _____?" He was supposed to meet me here. *(Keeps looking around for partner.)* "We were going to play a game. Maybe you've heard of it. It's called Busy Bee. I love that game." *(Keeps looking for partner.)* "But I don't see _____ here to play it on . . . I mean with. Hey, wait a minute. I'm a pretty smart clown. I bet I can figure out a way to play the game without him. I've got my chair right here . . . *(Looks back at water on floor)* and I'm all set. *(Turns to speak to imaginary Clown B)* Ahem. _____, wanna play a game? *(Switches places to become imaginary Clown B.)*

10

Clown B: What kind of game? *(Keeps switching back and forth to be in proper place for each clown's words.)*

Clown A: A really fun game.

Clown B: I guess I could play. What's it called? How do you play it?

Clown A: It's called Busy Bee. Now, see this chair?

Clown B: Yeah.

Clown A: Well, it's not really a chair. It's a throne. And you get to sit on it because you're the Queen Bee.

Clown B: On, no you don't. I'm not going to be a QUEEN.

Clown A: But that just means you're the boss—the ruler. Don't you wanna be the boss?

Clown B: Well all right, the ruler. Could I be a yardstick instead?

Clown A: No, you just be the ruler.

Clown B: Okay, but no funny stuff.

Clown A: Oh, no. Now you just sit here on your throne and get comfortable. Now, I'm the worker bee. I fly all over collecting honey. You do like honey, don't you?

Clown B: (Sitting on chair.) Oh, yes. I love honey.

Clown A: (Standing) Good. Then when I get back to

you, I'll go umuh, umuh, umuh *(or your own sound effect)*, and you say: "Busy bee, busy bee, what have you got in the hive for me?" Then I give it to you. See? Isn't that a fun and easy game?

Clown B: I guess so.

Clown A: Now you stay right here, and I'll go and gather the honey.

(Clown A moves around stage flapping wings and humming like a bee. Gets a mouthful of water from the glass behind the chair and comes up to stand alongside of chair. Clown A then makes sounds described above.)

Clown A: Umuh, Umuh, Umuh. *(Clown A sits in Clown B's chair, looking up at where Clown A was standing.)*

Clown B: Busy bee, busy bee, what have you got in the hive for me? *(As this line is spoken water spills out of clown's mouth.)*

Clown A: *(Stands)* Oh, I wet myself. That didn't work out too good. I'll have to try again. *(Clown A moves around stage as before and gets another mouthful of water.)*

Clown A: Umuh, Umuh, Umuh. *(Moves to sit in chair. Tries to say Clown B's lines out of side of the mouth, again with no luck. Finally, tilts head back and gargles out the line.)*

Clown B: *(Gargling)* Busy bee, busy bee, what have you got in the hive for me?

12

Clown A: *(Proud of successfully saying the line, stands up to spit water at the clown in chair. Realizes there's no one there, gestures frustration to the audience and contemplates a solution. Tries spitting a little water in the right direction, and sit in the chair before the water gets there, but sits too late. Finally, he gets an idea. While sitting in the chair, spit the water straight up in the air. Water comes back down on Clown A like a fountain. Stands up sputtering and wiping the water off.)*

Clown A: That was kind of stupid. I think next time I'll wait for _____. *(Exits, taking chair and water.)*

The End

Acknowledgement: This skit was developed and first performed by Jan "Macaroni" Bergesen at the 1994 World Clown Association Convention in Las Vegas.

CARPET LAYER

Number of Clowns: One

Characters: Carpet Layer

Costumes: Coveralls, such as a carpet installer would wear

Props: Paste bucket, large brush, rubber mallet, piece of (rigged) carpet approximately 30 inches by 5 feet (see note at end of skit)

Stage: Empty

The Performance

Clown enters carrying a piece of rolled up carpet over his shoulder. He "discovers" a hole in the stage floor, and decides to place the carpet over it. It looks like an easy job.

He puts the tools aside, and places the carpet on the floor. He then unrolls the carpet over the imaginary hole in floor. With the "simple" job completed, he stands back to take a look at it. He is surprised to find that one end (B) of the carpet is still sticking up in the air. He goes over and pushes it down. He looks at his work again, and is embarrassed to find that the first end (A) is now sticking up. He has a problem.

He nonchalantly walks over and pushes end "A" down with his foot. "B" comes up. He is now getting angry. He goes to end "B" and pushes it down with his foot, then stomps on it.

"A" comes up. He pulls himself back, standing on end "B", and dives for end "A" to push it back down. While lying on the carpet, he peeks back over his shoulder to see that "B" has again come up.

He tries to hold his foot on "A" and stretch the other foot to push "B" down, but just as his one foot reaches "B" the other foot comes off of "A" which pops back up.

He is now getting very angry. He gets the glue bucket, puts glue on the underside of "A" and pushes it down. He turns around, knowing that "B" is probably up. He goes to end "B", puts glue on its underside, and glues it down. Proud of his accomplishment, he gets up to survey his work.

He becomes furious as he discovers that end "A" is back up in the air. He gets his hammer and proceeds to hammer it down. He then nails end "B" down as well and gets up to see his completed job.

When he sees that "A" is up again, he drops the hammer. It hits his toe, and he dances around with a "sore" toe. He stops. He is very angry. He picks up his tools, rolls up the carpet, and limps off the stage.

The End

Note: Carpet piece is rigged with a steel bar across each end for weight. The ends are also connected with monofilament fish line to force one end to come up when the other end is pushed down. Other than this, all props are normal.

Acknowledgement: This skit is an adaptation of an old rodeo gag.

COOKING LESSON

Number of Clowns: One

Characters: Cook

Costumes: Cooking attire (apron, etc.)

Props: Card table, tableware, extra plates, cups and saucers, two vases with flowers (one large and one small), tablecloth, boom box, prerecorded cassette tape with all taped comments on it, small table for boom box

Stage: Table in center with table settings (large flowers in large vase, plates, and ugly table cloth), small table for boom box

Setting: Clown enters carrying box of dishes (table setting "kit") and boom box. Sets up boom box on table.

The Performance

Clown: Oh boy. I'm so happy. My correspondence course materials arrived and I'm anxious to see what's in it. *(Looks to audience.)* I have a big party coming up, and I sent away for some instructions on how to plan my party. *(Opens box of dishes.)* Hmmm. I guess I have to put this tape into my player for the instructions. *(Inserts tape into boom box and hits PLAY button, then steps back to the table.)*

Tape: Hello, and welcome to this series of lessons on HOW TO PLAN THE PERFECT PARTY. Your Party Planning Kit includes all the necessary items you will need for each lesson. Today we'll be talking about the proper way to set your party table. Before we can begin, you must first clear your table of everything that is on it.

16

Clown: *(Clears table by pushing everything off onto floor with one swing of the arm then continues to adjust gaudy table cloth, which remains.)*

Tape: Place your very nice party dishes on the table in this order. Step number one, the largest plate is placed directly in front of where each person will be sitting.

Clown: *(Removes large dinner plates from box and places four plates on the table.)*

Tape: Step two, the smaller plate is placed just above the larger plate, and slightly to the right.

Clown: *(Removes smaller plates from box and places them ON TOP of large plates.)*

Tape: Not on top of the large plates, silly. Place them above and to the right of the large plates.

Clown: *(Looks at radio, as if "how did you know?" then moves each smaller plate to the proper place.)*

Tape: That's better. Now, step three, find the cups in the box and place them on top of the smaller plates.

Clown: *(Gets cups out and places them accordingly.)*

Tape: Step four, now for the center-piece. A vase with flowers.

Clown: *(Picks up vase and large flower from floor to put it on the table.)*

Tape: No, not that one. For your party you'll want a smaller-size vase and flowers. It should be in your kit.

Take it out and place it in the center of your table.

Clown: *(Removes vase and flowers from kit and places them in the center of table.)*

Tape: Perfect. And that completes your table setting lesson for today. In our next lesson we'll discuss proper placement of napkins and eating utensils. Oh, I almost forgot. You should never use an ugly, atrocious table cloth, like the one you have, for special parties. If you haven't already removed the "pretty" table cloth from your kit, do it now. If you still have that ugly one on the table, please clear your table and start over at step number one. I hope you've enjoyed this tape and remember, no ugly tablecloths.

Clown: *(Holds up a pretty table cloth, looks at it, and looks at the one on the table. Looks surprised at what the tape says, and comes up with another idea. Grasps one edge of the tablecloth by the side and pulls it quickly to remove it, with all dishes remaining on the table, then walks proudly from stage.)*

The End

Acknowledgement: This is based on a skit written by Ruth Matteson and performed at the 1993 World Clown Association Convention in Merrillville, Indiana.

DOVE IN THE BAG

Number of Clowns: One
Characters: Clown
Costumes: Regular clown wardrobe
Props: Paper sandwich bag filled with yellow feathers
Stage: Empty

The Performance

Clown enters the stage talking about the great magic production that he is going to present. Clown explains that most great magicians can produce animals, and that is what he is going to do. He asks audience what kind of animals magicians produce. There will be various answers, but the one you are looking for is "BIRD." When the clown has made it apparent that he will produce a bird in the bag, he solicits the aid of the audience in saying the magic words. Before saying the magic words, air is blown into the gag to give the bird some "air to breath." This prepares the bag to be popped later. Magician will say the magic words first, and audience repeats them as follows:

Clown: Abracadabra.

Audience: Abracadabra.

Clown: Peace and love.

Audience: Peace and love.

Clown: Into the bag.

Audience: Into the bag.

Clown: Appear a dove.

Audience: Appear a dove.

Clown looks into bag, looks at the audience and explains to the audience that "it isn't that big of a trick. Maybe we'll have to produce a smaller bird." He tries again, blowing some air into bag between saying the magic words.

Clown: Abracadabra.

Audience: Abracadabra.

Clown: Just a smidgen.

Audience: Just a smidgen.

Clown: Into the bag.

Audience: Into the bag.

Clown: Appear a pigeon.

Audience: Appear a pigeon.

Clown looks into bag, looks at the audience and explains to the audience that "it still isn't that big of a trick. Maybe we'll have to produce a smaller bird." He tries again, this time blowing more air into the bag as he says the magic words.

Clown: Abracadabra.

Audience: Abracadabra.

Clown: Fuzzy and hairy.

Audience: Fuzzy and hairy.

Clown: Into the bag.

Audience: Into the bag.

Clown: Appear a canary.

Audience: Appear a canary.

Clown is excited and happy. He claps his hands together over the bag as the audience watches. Naturally, he breaks the bag and yellow feathers fall to the floor. Clown looks surprised and embarrassed at having ruined the imaginary bird. Audience is laughing as clown picks up feathers and leaves stage.

The End

> *Note:* If you are concerned about leaving little children with the impression that you killed the canary, you can produce another one as you attempt to pick up the feathers from the floor and show the children that the canary was okay after all. This is not necessary with adult audiences.

ESP - MINDREADER #1

Number of Clowns: One

Characters: Clown

Costumes: Regular clown wardrobe

Props: Cards with line drawings of: an animal (stick figure that could represent any number of animals), a stick person, the word "NO", and a bar code (UPC symbol)

Stage: Empty

Setting: Clown enters stage explaining that he is a world famous psychic (mindreader) and that he has already read the minds of several members of the audience.

The Performance ━━━━━━━━━━━━━━━

(Clown enters stage, greets audience.) Ladies and Gentlemen. It is my extreme pleasure to be here tonight and to exhibit my exceptional skills in the art of reading minds. I thought this would be a rather easy task this evening, but after waiting backstage trying to read some of your minds, I think it's going to be harder than I thought.

I have, in this envelope, some predetermined outcomes to what you are thinking. *(Picks up large manila envelope that is closed. Inside the envelope is a stick drawing of an animal.)*

Let's see. This envelope is titled "Animal," so that means it will reveal an animal that someone in this audience is thinking of. Can I see the hand of a volunteer who is thinking, or will think, of an animal. It can be any animal of your choice, exotic, wild, or tame. The only stipulation is that it must be an animal. *(Selects someone from audience.)*

Thank you for volunteering. Are you thinking of an animal? *(Volunteer probably says "Yes.")*

Will you tell everyone here, and me, just what animal you are thinking of. *(Volunteer names an animal.)*

(The clown appears astonished.) That's amazing. It is the exact animal that I have already drawn and placed in this envelope. Thank you very much. Let's have a nice hand for our volunteer. *(Audience will probably object since they have not seen animal drawing.)*

Oh, you don't believe me. You want to see the drawing. Well okay. *(He removes the drawing of the stick figure and shows audience that it is the animal the volunteer selected.)*

I feel there are some skeptics among you. I'll try to eliminate your doubts by doing something else. *(Picks up new envelope.)*

In this envelope I have a picture of a very famous person, who is either living or dead. I can't reveal it to you until our audience volunteer picks the person. May I have another volunteer? *(He selects an audience member, has him stand, and introduces him.)*

Thank you for volunteering. Are you thinking of a

famous person? *(Audience member responds.)*

Is the person living or deceased? *(Audience member responds.)*

Do you think I have a picture of the person you've selected? *(Audience member probably says, "No.")*

(Clown takes the "NO" card from the envelope.) You are exactly right, and I predicted it.

But wait. You haven't revealed the name of the person you selected. What is the name of your person? *(Audience member responds.)*

(Clown removes stick drawing of person and holds it with the back of the card facing the audience.)

That's amazing. I have a picture of that very person right here. Let me show it to you. *(He turns the picture around to show audience, and probably receives many groans.)*

I have just one more prediction, and this one is very difficult. It can not be represented by stick drawings. This next prediction must be an exact number, which I cannot even know at this time. I will need one last volunteer. *(Selects volunteer, gets name as above, etc.)*

Now, I'd like you to pretend that you are visiting a large grocery store doing your weekly shopping. You can be in any aisle you desire, but I'd like you to give me the name of one product you will purchase. *(Volunteer names a product.)*

Now, that particular item may come in various sizes. I don't know which size you prefer, so please tell me the size of the item you have selected. *(Volunteer names a size.)*

And now for the last, and most important piece of information. The price. I'm sure the price is displayed on the shelf with the product. Since I had no prior knowledge of the product you would select, or the size of the product, wouldn't it be amazing if I have preselected the exact price of your item? *(Volunteer responds.)*

Now what is the exact price of your item? *(Volunteer responds.)*

This is great. Even I am surprised that I predicted it to the exact penny and have it written on this card. Let me show you my prediction. *(Clown turns card over displaying wide and narrow lines of UPC pricing code.)*

(Clown takes bows as audience applauds and groans with appreciation.)

The End

SUCKERS ON THE LINE

Number of Clowns: One
Characters: Clown who receives telephone call
Costumes: Regular clown wardrobe
Props: Telephone
Stage: Table with telephone on it

The Performance

(Clown enters stage, greets audience.) Hello, everybody.
I'm so glad you are able to be with us today and to visit
our candy store. *(Telephone rings.)*

Excuse me. Let me get that telephone. *(Clown answers
phone)* Hello? *(Pauses for answer.)* Hello? *(Pause)*
Hello? *(Pause)* It seems that there's something wrong
with my telephone line. Can I get a volunteer from the
audience to help me with it? *(Looks to the audience for
a volunteer. Finds one and brings that person onto the
stage.)*

Thank you so very much for volunteering to help me.
Just hop right up onto the stage. *(Volunteer enters
stage.)*

*(Positions volunteer facing audience, with both arms up
over head. Places wire from phone in each hand so that
the wire proceeds across stage.)*

That's wonderful. Now, let me see who's trying to call
me. Hello? *(Waits for answer.)* Hello? *(Pause)* Hello?
(Pause) This phone still doesn't work. I think you need

some more help. *(Goes to audience again, gets another volunteer. Brings this person onto stage, positions him next to first person, both with arms in air, and puts telephone wire in each hand. Clown now has two people facing the audience, each holding the telephone wire as it proceeds across stage.)*

(Clown tries phone again) Hello? *(Waits for an answer.)* Hello? *(Pause)* Hello? *(Pause)*

Ya know, it still doesn't work. I think we need some more help. *(Goes to audience again, gets another volunteer. Brings this person onto the stage positions him next to others, all with arms in the air and telephone wire in each hand. Clown now has three people facing the audience, each holding the telephone wire.)*

Let me try it now. Hello? *(Waits for answer.)* Hello? *(Pause)* Hello? *(Pause)* It still isn't working. *(Looks down the line past the volunteers who are holding the line up in the air.)* There seems to be a slight sag in between two of you. I think I need a real tall person to help me there, then everything will probably work just right. *(Clown goes to audience again, selects a tall volunteer. This person is placed into the line just as the others.)*

Now it looks just right. Let me try it again. Hello? *(Waits briefly for answer.)* Oh, yeah. I can hear you just fine. This is the candy shop. What can I do for you? No, I don't have those kind of lollipops, but I've got four suckers on the line. *(Clown takes line back from volunteers and helps them from the stage, then exits.)*

The End

BABY BILL

Number of Clowns: Two

Characters: Clown with baby (Clown A), clown pest (Clown B)

Costumes: Regular clown wardrobe

Props: Blanket rolled up to resemble a baby being held in arms

Stage: Chair downstage center

Setting: Clown A enters carrying a blanket with "baby" wrapped up in it. He is playing with the baby, making baby sounds, talking to it, and making baby crying sounds, if possible. He walks around downstage momentarily, sticks his thumb in baby's mouth, and baby stops crying. He quickly pulls thumb out and looks at it as if baby bit him. Clown A sits down.

The Performance

Clown B: *(Enters upstage. He is happy.)* Whatcha got there?

Clown A: What d'ya think I got here? I got a baby. *(Makes more baby sounds.)*

Clown B: Can I see your baby? *(Tries to stand behind the chair to see it. Clown A keeps moving the baby so Clown B can not see it.)*

Clown A: No. You can't see my baby.

Clown B: Aw. Let me see your baby.

Clown A: No. It's my baby.

Clown B: I wanna see your baby.

Clown A: You can't see my baby. *(Clown B moves around the chair to see the baby. Clown A gets up and moves away.)*

Clown B: Let me see your baby. *(Clown B sits on the chair.)*

Clown A: Hey, hey, careful. It's a heavy baby.

Clown B: What's that baby's name?

Clown A: That baby's name is . . . ah . . . ah . . . *(Looks at the baby.)* What's your name? *(Looks up, pauses)* Bill.

Clown B: Bill?

Clown A: Yeah. His name is Bill. What are you bugging me for? *(Both clowns are walking around on stage with Clown B always upstage trying to get a peek at the baby, and Clown A shielding the baby from view.)*

Clown B: I wanna see that baby Bill.

Clown A: Why do you want to see this baby? You were a baby once, don't you remember what you looked like?

Clown B: Let me see that baby Bill.

Clown A: It's my baby Bill

Clown B: How come I can't see that baby Bill?

Clown A: You can't see the baby. It's my baby Bill.

Clown B: *(Pleading)* Let me see your baby.

Clown A: I'm the only one that can see Bill.

Clown B: Why?

Clown A: *(Unrolls blanket he had in his arms revealing that there was no baby, just the blanket.)* Because he's invisi-Bill. *(Clown B chases Clown A offstage.)*

The End

Acknowledgement: This skit was developed by Ron Kardynski for a graduation show presented by Clown Antics, Westland, Michigan.

BANANA BANDANNA

Number of Clowns: Two
Characters: Clown Magician, Stooge
Costumes: Regular clown wardrobe
Props: Yellow bandanna, banana
Stage: Empty

The Performance

Clown: *(Clown enters stage.)* Boy, I sure hope
_____ is not around. *(Reaches into pocket.)*
Because, I've got a magic trick I want to do.

Stooge: *(Enters from upstage.)* Hi _____.

Clown: *(Exasperated and surprised.)* Hi _____.
(Looks back and waves.)

Stooge: *(Walks across stage in back of Clown.)*

Clown: *(Speaking to audience.)* Whew, boy! That was
close. I've got a new magic trick I want to show you.

Stooge: *(Was just about to leave upstage, but had not
left the stage yet. He turns around and looks at Clown.
Takes a step in that direction as if Clown was talking to
him when saying "want to show you.")* You wanna show
me a magic trick?

Clown: No!

Stooge: That's what you said.

Clown: No. Not you.

Stooge: P-l-e-a-s-e.

Clown: No. You never do anything right. No.

Stooge: Please. Won't you just show me? *(Turns to audience.)* Don't you think he should show me how to do the magic trick? *(Waits for audience reaction.)*

Clown: *(Throws his arms up in the air admitting defeat.)* All right. All right. I'll show you how to do it, but you gotta promise you'll stand back there *(gestures to back of stage)*, and be quiet and don't bother me. Okay?

Stooge: Okay.

Clown: Now go and stand back there.

Stooge: *(Moves to upstage spot.)* How's this?

Clown: That's good. Now you gotta have a bandanna. *(Takes yellow bandanna from pocket.)*

Stooge: Oh, wait. *(Looks into pockets.)* I don't have one.

Clown: Well, go over there to my case *(points off stage)* and get one. I have a bunch of yellow ones there.

Stooge: *(Goes quickly to side of stage and gets yellow banana from case. Returns to upstage position on stage.)* I've got one. I'm ready now. *(Proudly)*

Note: It is important that, from this point on, Clown does not turn to look at Stooge.

Clown: You've gotta have a bandanna *(holds it up)* and a quarter. *(Takes quarter from pocket.)*

Stooge: *(Reaches into pocket and takes out quarter.)* I've got both of them. I'm ready.

Clown: I want you to take your bandanna *(holds bandanna up in front of her)*.

Stooge: *(Holds up banana to show the audience)* I've got my bandanna.

Clown: Open it up. *(Unfolds bandanna.)*

Stooge: Open it up. *(Peels banana.)*

Clown: And show everybody that there's nothing in it. *(Holds unfolded bandanna, turns it back to front and back again to show audience it's empty.)*

Stooge: *(Shows peeled banana to the audience.)* There's nothing in my bandanna.

Clown: I want you to take your bandanna and fold the right top corner to the bottom left corner.

Stooge: *(Holding banana horizontally in hands.)* The right top corner to the bottom left corner? *(Looks quizzically at Clown in front, wondering if he's doing it right.)*

Clown: Yep. The right top to the left bottom. Now, take the left top corner and fold it to the right bottom.

Stooge: The left top to the right bottom. *(By now, Stooge is just squeezing banana into a ball in his hands.)*

Clown: Now again, to make it smaller, the right top to the left bottom.

Stooge: *(Follows along, squeezing banana even more.)*

Clown: And the left top to the right bottom.

Stooge: *(Squeezes again, looking proud.)* I'm doing magic.

Clown: *(Holds bandanna in palm of hand.)* Now, you make a hole right in the middle of your bandanna. *(Sticks thumb into bandanna to make hole.)*

Stooge: I make a hole in the middle?

Clown: Yeah.

Stooge: Right in the middle? (Sticks thumb into the middle of the banana.)

Clown: Yeah, right in the middle. Then you take your quarter. *(Takes quarter from pocket and holds it up.)*

Stooge: *(Holds up his quarter.)* I got my quarter. I'm really doing it. I'm doing magic. *(Appears proud.)* I'm doing good.

Clown: And you put your quarter into the hole in the bandanna.

Stooge: *(Puts quarter into hole in banana.)*

Clown: Now take it . . .

Stooge: Yeah?

Clown: And put it in your pocket.

Stooge: *(Looks around inquisitively, as if he didn't hear correctly. Continues to look at Clown and at audience)* Take it and . . . ? *(Stops and again looks at Clown as if asking "are you serious?")*

Clown: Put it in your pocket.

Stooge: Is this a real magic trick?

Clown: *(Pauses)* Yeah, it's a real magic trick. Now, put it in your pocket. Ready?

Stooge: Wait a minute. *(Hesitantly puts banana into pocket.)*

> *Note:* Stooge should have a plastic bag inside his pocket so he doesn't ruin the costume.

Stooge: *(The banana is pushed into his pocket.)* Okay. I'm ready.

Clown: *(Turns to look at Stooge. This is the first time Clown has looked at Stooge since the beginning of the trick.)* Come up here by me. (Stooge comes to front of stage and stands next to Clown.) Now. You have to hit your pocket.

Stooge: What?

Clown: You have to hit it three times like this . . . *(Hits own pocket three times, counting as she hits)* one . . . two . . . three.

Stooge: *(Steps away from Clown slightly and looks around at the audience, giving the impression he doesn't want to do this.)* Now, wait a minute. I went along with showing everybody there was nothing inside of my bandanna, and I went along with folding my bandanna, and I went along with putting a little hole, in it and putting a quarter into the hole and I even went along with putting it into my pocket.

Clown: Yeah, you did all of that stuff like you're supposed to do.

Stooge: But I'm not gonna hit my pocket three times.

Clown: It's easy. Just like this. *(Hits own pocket three times.)* That's what makes teh magic. If you don't do it, I will.

Stooge: I'm not gonna hit it.

Clown: Then I will. *(Hits Stooge's pocket three times.)* One . . . two . . . three.

Stooge: *(Reacts squeamishly.)*

Clown: Now, take it out of your pocket . . . *(Removes bandanna from own pocket, while Stooge attempts to take banana from his own pocket. Clown unfolds bandanna and holds it up for audience to see.)*

Stooge: *(Still trying to take banana mess out of his pocket.)*

Clown: And show everybody that your quarter has disappeared.

Stooge: *(Takes the quarter from the banana mess and holds it up.)* My quarter is still here.

Clown: *(Looks at Stooge, and the mess in his hands.)* What is that?

Stooge: That's my bandanna with a quarter.

Clown: That's not a bandanna, that's a banana.
_____, you can't do anything right. *(They chase each other off stage.)*

The End

Acknowledgement: This was first performed by Anita Dopp and Marti Vast Binder at the 1984 Midwest Clown Association Convention in Merrillville, Indiana. It won first place in skit competition.

BROOM SWING

Number of Clowns: Two

Characters: Clown A, Clown B

Costumes: Normal clown wardrobe with suspenders

Props: Two brooms

Stage: Empty

The Performance

Clowns enter stage from opposite sides. They are "backing" onto the stage and sweeping while working their way toward the center of the stage. Moving rather slowly, they finally get to center stage, and gently "back" into each other. They look to the right (both to the right, so they are not looking at each other), then to the left. They then rotate (backs touching) counterclockwise half-way around. They are now facing the opposite direction, with backs still touching. They are sweeping slightly while doing the above. Clown A pretends to see a fly in the air and swats at it with his broom. He swats in front of himself a couple times. Then, without looking, he swats over his head, and over the head of Clown B, who has bent down to pick up a speck of dirt from the floor. (TIMING IS IMPORTANT.) They each turn toward the audience and discover each other. They react with emotion, dropping their brooms, jumping back, and screaming with surprise as they become aware that there is another sweeper.

Clown A: *(After calming down.)* You scared me! *(Slaps Clown B three times—left hand, right hand, left hand.)*

Clown B: *(Reacts to slaps from Clown A, staggers around.)*

Clown A: Don't do that again or I'll have to do this. *(Moves hand back and forth quickly in front of Clown B's face, as if slapping him side to side. Clown B reacts by moving his head back and forth as if being hit, then again staggers toward audience.)*

Clown B: Oh yeah? *(He takes Clown A by his suspenders and bounces him up and down. Clown B is lifting the suspenders and Clown A is actually jumping to create the illusion that he is being bounced up and down.)*

Clown A: *(Takes Clown B's suspenders and tries to move Clown B up and down. Clown B just stands there, with Clown A only moving suspenders up and down.)*

Clown B: Hey. Let's work together and be a team. Okay?

Clown A: All right. That sounds good to me. *(They both bend to pick up the brooms and collide. They get up, look at each other and try again.)*

Clown B: Let's pick them up on the count of three.

Clown A: On three.

Clown B: One, two, three. *(They bend to pick up the brooms and hit their heads together. One of them makes a noise which sounds like heads hitting. They stagger.)*

Clown B: Hey. Let's pick 'em up on four, instead.

Clown A: Okay. FOUR! *(Clown A picks up broom in both hands, holding it horizontally in front of him. When he is upright, with broom, he appears to be looking around and makes half turn in counterclockwise direction. Clown B is standing to his right, reaching down to pick up his broom. As a result of Clown A's turn, Clown B gets hit in butt.)*

Clown B: Oh, ow!

Clown A: *(Turns back, accidently hitting Clown B in his stomach with other end of the broom.)*

Clown B: *(Bends forward when hit with the broom. Clown A lifts his broom, hitting Clown B in the face as he is bent over. Clown B straightens up and turns to his right, away from Clown A.)*

Clown A: *(Makes another counterclockwise turn, again hitting Clown B in the butt.)*

Clown B: *(Does a forward roll and lays on the floor.)*

Clown A: *(Moves over toward Clown B.)* Hey, I shouldn't be doing all the work. *(Picks up Clown B's broom.)*

Clown B: *(Gets up, sees that Clown A has both brooms and fears that Clown A is about to hit him with both. He runs off stage, with Clown A running after him.)*

The End

Acknowledgement: Most of the outline for this skit was developed by Jose Rivera and Bob Ammon at a Just Say No, Clown-In at Knoxville, Tennessee.

BUSY BEE (TWO-PERSONS)

Number of Clowns: Two

Characters: Clown A, Clown B

Costumes: Regular clown wardrobe

Props: Chair and glass of water

Stage: Chair downstage center, glass of water on floor behind the chair

Setting: Clown A enters looking for partner. Calls for partner, looks to each side of the stage still calling for the other clown.

The Performance

Clown A: *(Looks at audience.)* Have you seen _____? He was supposed to meet me here. *(Continues to look around for partner.)* We were going to play a game. Maybe you've heard of it. It's called Busy Bee. I love that game. *(Still looking for partner.)* But I don't see _____ here to play it on . . . I mean with.

Clown B: *(Enters the stage looking around, not noticing Clown A already present.)*

Clown A: Ahem. Hey _____, wanna play a game?

Clown B: What kind of game?

Clown A: A really fun game.

Clown B: I guess I could play. What's it called? How do you play it?

Clown A: It's called Busy Bee. Now, see this chair?

Clown B: Yeah.

Clown A: Well it's not really a chair. It's a throne. And you get to sit on it because you're the Queen Bee.

Clown B: On, no you don't. I'm not going to be a QUEEN.

Clown A: But that just means you're the boss—the ruler. Don't you wanna be the boss?

Clown B: Well all right, the ruler. Could I be a yard-stick instead?

Clown A: No, you just be the ruler.

Clown B: Okay, but no funny stuff.

Clown A: Oh, no. Now you just sit here on your throne and get comfortable. Now, I'm the worker bee. I fly all over collecting honey. You do like honey, don't you?

Clown B: Oh yes, I love honey.

Clown A: Good. Then when I get back to you, I'll go umuh, umuh, umuh *(or some other sound effect),* and you say, "Busy bee, busy bee, what have you got in the hive for me?" And then I give it to you. Sec? Isn't that a fun and easy game?

Clown B: I guess so.

Clown A: Now you stay right here, and I'll go and gather the honey. *(Clown A flies around gathering the honey, gets a mouthful of water from the glass, and returns)* Umuh, umuh, umuh.

Clown B: Busy bee, busy bee, what have you got in the hive for me?

Clown A: *(Spits mouthful of water on Clown B.)*

Clown B: *(Stands up embarrassed and upset.)* I don't like this game. I'm not going to play it anymore.

Clown A: Oh, let's play it one more time, but this time you can be the worker bee.

Clown B: *(Thinks it over.)* Well, okay. I think I can do that. *(Winks to audience to indicate he will be playing the trick on Clown A.)*

Clown A: I'll sit right here and be the Queen Bee. You fly around and get the honey.

Clown B: Okay. *(Flies around as Clown A did and gathers the honey, including getting a mouthful of water* *from glass behind chair. He comes up to the side of chair.)* Umuh, umuh, umuh.

Clown A: *(Does not respond. Just looks around room oblivious to Clown B's presence.)*

Clown B: *(Louder and more emphatic.)* Umuh, umuh, umuh.

Clown A: *(Sits there looking around, looks at Clown B but still does not respond.)*

Clown B: *(Swallows water.)* Hey, you're not playing fair. You're supposed to say "Busy bee, busy bee, what have you got in the hive for me?"

Clown A: Oh, I'm sorry. I guess I forgot. I'll do it right this time.

Clown B: Well okay. I'll try again. *(Flies around again and gets more water. Comes back to side of chair.)* Umuh, umuh, umuh.

Clown A: *(Ignores Clown B.)*

Clown B: *(Gets very angry and swallows water.)* I'm not playing anymore. You don't play fair.

Clown A: Oh, let's try one more time. I must have been thinking of something else.

Clown B: Well, only one more time. And you better get it right this time.

Clown A: I'll be very careful to do it right.

46

Clown B: *(As before, he goes around flying, gathering honey, and gets mouthful of water. But while Clown B is flying around, Clown A turns around and gets mouthful of water from the glass. Clown B returns to side of chair.)* Umuh, Umuh, Umuh.

Clown A: *(Ignores B again.)*

Clown B: *(Very upset and swallows the water.)* You're supposed to say, "Busy-bee, busy-bee, what have you got in the hive for me?"

Clown A: *(Gets up, stands on chair, and spits water at Clown B.)* I've played this game before and I knew what to do. Isn't it fun?

Clown B: I never did like this game. I'm getting out of here. *(Runs off stage.)*

The End

Acknowledgement: I first saw this skit performed by Leon "Buttons" McBryde and Earl "Mr. Clown" Chaney.

47

CLOWN SHOOT-OUT

Number of Clowns: Two

Characters: Shooting Machine (Clown), Stooge

Costumes: Normal clown wardrobe

Props: Two toy guns

Stage: Shooting Machine (Clown) is standing on stage (or walks out and takes position near center stage)

Setting: Stooge enters. Sees Shooting Machine and decides to investigate.

The Performance

Clown: Clown shoot-out. Only 25 cents. Clown shoot-out. Only 25 cents.

Stooge: *(Deposits coin into the machine and steps back.)*

Clown: Ding! Welcome to the shoot-out. Remove gun from under foot. Walk back three paces, coun to three, turn around, and fire.

Stooge: *(Removes gun from under Clown's foot, turns around and starts to walk three paces.)*

Clown: *(Counting as Stooge walks.)* One . . . two . . . *(before Stooge gets into position to turn around)* THREE! Bang! Bang! You're dead. You lost. Please place gun back under my foot.

Stooge: *(Surprised, but puts gun under foot and looks at the machine.)*

Clown: *(Waits until gun is under his foot.)* Clown shoot-out. Only 25 cents. Clown shoot-out. Only 25 cents.

Stooge: *(Deposits coin.)*

Clown: Ding! Welcome to the shoot out. Remove gun from under foot. Walk back three paces and count to three, then turn around and fire.

Stooge: *(Tries to remove gun from under Clown A's foot. but the gun is stuck. The Clown's foot presses down so hard that Stooge cannot remove it.)*

Clown: One . . . two . . . three. Bang! Bang! You're dead. You lost. Please place gun back under my foot. Clown shoot-out. Only 25 cents. Clown shoot-out. Only 25 cents

Stooge: *(Frustrated, he manages to remove the gun from under Clown's foot. Deposits coin and points gun at Clown.)*

Clown: Welcome to Clown shoot-out. Remove gun from under foot. Walk back three paces, count to three, turn around, and fire. One . . . t-w-o . . . *(Clown stops at "two" as if run down.)*

Stooge: *(Disgusted, puts gun back under Clown's foot.)*

Clown: Three! Bang! Bang! You're dead. You lost. Please place gun back under my foot.   Clown shoot-out. Only 25 cents. Clown shoot-out. Only 25 cents.

(Stooge tries to shake machine. Seems to dislodge Clown and set him off-balance. Clown regains balance. Stooge

now realizes that Clown A is really a person, and that he has been tricked.)

Stooge: Hey. You're not a machine. You're a person and you're been taking my money.

Clown: That's right, friend. Thanks for the donations. *(Starts to run away.)*

Stooge: *(Chases Clown from the stage.)*

The End

Acknowledgement: To the best of my knowledge, this skit was developed by the San Diego Stage University Clown Club. It was presented by the club at the 1989 World Clown Association Convention in San Diego.

DEAD AND ALIVE

Number of Clowns: Two
Characters: Clown A, Clown B
Costumes: Normal clown wardrobe
Props: Hats
Stage: Empty

The Performance

Clown A enters empty stage and begins picking imaginary flowers, not paying any attention to the audience. He might be whistling or humming. Clown B enters, sees Clown A and tries to get his attention. He puts his upstage hand to his mouth and hollers, "HEY!"

When Clown A sees him, they both face each other, put arms out to the sides, and say "welcome" with their gesture. They are still 20 feet apart. Next, they both turn to face the audience, pointing their arms at their friend to gesture to the audience that "this is my friend."

They face each other again and move toward each other, stopping about three feet apart. Clown B puts his hand out to shake hands, while Clown A lifts his hat as a gesture of greeting. They change their greeting, with Clown A now reaching to shake and Clown B lifting his hat. They continue reversing their actions about eight or ten times, never getting it together. Clown A steps away while Clown B continues alternating between attempting to shake hands and lifting his hat upward. He goes faster and faster as he tries. Clown A walks about 10-15 feet away watching Clown B go through these motions, and gesturing to the audience that Clown B must be crazy.

Clown A goes back to Clown B and stomps on his foot. Clown B stops shaking, bends his knee to raise his foot upward, grabs his foot, and dances around while making sounds of pain. He does about one complete turn, moaning and dancing. Clown A, watching, thinks Clown B is just dancing, and he begins to dance too. Clown B stops dancing, puts his foot down, and watches Clown A dancing across the stage.

Clown B approaches Clown A and gently taps him on the shoulder to stop him from dancing. He continues to dance. Clown B taps harder with no effect. He then slaps Clown A with his upstage hand. Clown A drops backward and falls to the floor, face up, arms spread out to the sides and feet together.

Clown B is ready to leave. He gestures to Clown A to get up and go with him. Clown A just lies there. Clown B gestures two more times, but gets no response from Clown A. He becomes upset and figures that maybe Clown A cannot get up.

Clown B looks at Clown A, goes over to him, picks up his hat and begins fanning him to revive him. Clown A just lies there. Clown B gets down on the floor to listen for Clown A's heartbeat. Clown B gets up, sees that Clown A's arms are spread out. Clown B moves around and puts one foot on each side of Clown A's head, bends over, and moves Clown A's arms down to his sides. As he is doing this, Clown A's feet come apart about three feet. Clown B sees this, runs around to Clown A's feet, grabs each foot and moves the feet together. As he does this, Clown A's arms move back out into the original position. Clown B looks up, sees this, and runs back to Clown A's head. He reaches down and again moves Clown A's arms back to his sides. Again Clown A's feet spread apart.

Frustrated, Clown B pauses, and gets an idea. Clown B steps past Clown A's head and stands with one foot on each side of Clown A's arms to hold them in. He reaches down and closes Clown A's legs. As he does this, Clown A sits up, hitting B in the butt with his head. Clown B does a forward roll and ends up standing, facing Clown A, ready to fight.

Clown A is now sitting on the floor, arms at his sides, feet on the floor, but upper torso is sitting up. Clown B comes back, stepping with one leg on each side of Clown A. He pushes Clown A's shoulders to the floor. As he does this, Clown A's feet come up and kick Clown B in the butt. Clown B now does a forward dive over Clown A's head and ends up laying face down on the floor.

Clown A is now laying with his back on the floor and feet pointing to the ceiling. Clown B comes back. He stands behind Clown A and pushes Clown A's feet down. As he does this, Clown A's head comes up. (He is locked in an "L" position.) Clown B continues pushing Clown A's feet down while his head comes up, then pulling the feet back up to make the head go down. Finally Clown B gets an idea.

Clown B places his right foot on Clown A's chest and pushes Clown A's feet down. Clown A is now laying prone on the floor again, feet about 15 inches apart. Clown B goes to Clown A's head, puts both hands under Clown A's neck and proceeds to lift Clown A into an upright position. (It is important for Clown A to maintain a rigid position during this lift. It is also important that Clown A keep his feet about 15 inches apart for stability.)

After Clown B has his friend standing, he attempts to dust him off. While doing so, he realizes that Clown A's hat is on the floor behind them. Clown B knows he must get his friend's hat to put it on his head, but if he lets go, Clown A will probably fall. (This is the illusion that must be conveyed to the audience.)

Clown B decides to briefly let go of Clown A so as to reach back to get the hat. When he does, Clown A starts to fall backward before Clown B can get the hat. Clown B must turn quickly and catch Clown A before he falls. He tries again, with the same results.

Clown B now gets another idea. He quickly lays down on the floor in back of Clown A and puts his feet up to catch his friend's back as he begins to fall. After Clown A has landed on clown B's feet, Clown B can lower Clown A down, reach back and get the hat and place it hat on Clown A's head. Clown B can now quickly push Clown A up, with his feet, and again get Clown A into a standing position. Clown B quickly gets up to hold Clown A in a standing position. (See note at end for procedure on falling and catching.)

Now that Clown A is standing, with hat on, Clown B goes around to the front and gestures for Clown A to follow him. Since Clown A appears to be "dead," he does not respond. Clown B tries two more times to get Clown A to follow, with no luck. Clown B is now frustrated and goes back to Clown A.

Clown B hits Clown A in his stomach, causing Clown A to bend forward at the middle. Clown B goes behind Clown A and kicks him in the butt. Clown A now falls forward onto his hands and lowers his head to the floor in a three-point stance. Clown B picks up Clown A's feet, spreads his legs apart, turns around so that Clown B's back is now to Clown A's upside down front and steps between Clown A's legs.

Clown B pushes down, quickly, on Clown A's legs, causing Clown A to come up off the floor and be sitting on Clown B's back (since Clown B is now bent over forward). Clown B takes a few steps with Clown A on his back, waving his hat. Then Clown B stands up and Clown A slides from his back. Standing, they take final bows.

The End

Note: There must be a signal between the two clowns when they are doing the fall-backs. Just before turning to look for the hat, Clown B squeezes Clown A's shoulder. He then turns to retrieve hat. Clown A counts to ONE before starting to fall backward. The shoulder squeeze is the signal for the first two falls. More time is needed for the third fall, when Clown B is going to get on his back, with feet in the air. This time when Clown B squeezes Clown A's shoulder, Clown A counts to THREE before starting to fall. This gives Clown B time to get into position to catch Clown A on his feet.

Acknowledgement: I first saw this performed by Steve Smith and Earl Chaney at Clown Camp in 1983. Steve is a former director of Ringling Brothers and Barnum & Bailey Clown College, and Earl is a successful clown and entertainer in Las Vegas.

DISAPPEARING WATER

Number of Clowns: Two

Characters: Magician, Assistant

Costumes: Regular clown wardrobe (Magician can have a cape)

Props: Small table, pitcher of water, plastic glass, magic wand

Stage: Empty

The Performance

Magician enters carrying magic wand, and explains to the audience that he is going to perform an amazing magic trick that they have never seen before—he will make a glass of water disappear, without drinking it. Magician calls for his Assistant to bring the special props onto the stage. Assistant enters carrying tray (small table) with pitcher of water and glass. Tray is set near the center of the stage, and Assistant steps back to watch the trick. Magician proceeds to partially fill the glass with water, showing the audience that he is actually pouring the water into the glass. He sets the glass of water on the table and steps in front of the table to explain to the audience what is going to happen.

Magician speaks to the audience: "Ladies and gentlemen. You have seen me pour the water into the glass. Now I will say the magic words. Hocus pocus golly gee whiz, I wonder where the water is? I will then wave my magic want over the glass and the water will have mysteriously disappeared." While he is saying this to the audience, Assistant takes the glass from the table, drinks the water, and replaces the empty glass on the table.

Magician returns to the back of the table, prepared to do the trick. He starts to say, "Hocus pocus golly . . ." and notices the glass is empty. He looks bewildered, thinking that he already poured the water into the glass, but not really sure that he did. "Maybe I forgot to put the water into the glass. So, we'll try it again."

He again pours the water into the glass, steps in front of the table and goes through the same explanation. While he is doing this, Assistant again drinks the water, but this time replaces the glass upside down on the table.

Magician returns to the back of the table, starts to wave the wand over the glass and begins to say the magic words only to be surprised to see that the water is missing. He looks suspiciously at his Assistant, and asks the audience if his Assistant had anything to do with the missing water.

Assistant claims innocence, and Magician reluctantly picks up the glass and pours the water. He does not notice immediately that the glass is upside down and the water runs all over the outside of the glass. Magician jumps back looks suspiciously at Assistant, again. Turns glass right side up and fills it with water

Magician turns to Assistant, "Now you stay way over there, so that you won't be messing with my water." Assistant moves a little farther from the table.

The Magician again goes to the front of the table and explains the magic words and procedures. Assistant takes the glass from the table and drinks the water. This time, however, Assistant does not swallow the water.

Magician returns to the table, starts the trick and again notices the water is missing. He walks over to the Assistant and accuses him of taking the water. Assistant shakes head no. Magician asks audience if Assistant took the water. (Audience may say "yes" or "no" depending on the crowd.) In either case, the magician is sure the Assistant took the water.

"I want my water back," the Magician demands. Assistant shakes head, indicating he doesn't have the water.

"I said, I want my water returned." Assistant shrugs shoulders and shakes head no. "I want my water back RIGHT NOW! These are the key words for Assistant to react. Assistant sprays water into face of Magician. Magician is upset, looks at assistant, picks up the table with props and chases Assistant off the stage.

The End

ESP - MINDREADER #2

Number of Clowns: Two

Characters: Mindreader clown, clown Master of Ceremonies (MC)

Costumes: Turban and cape for Mindreader, regular clown wardrobe for MC

Props: Small blackboard and piece of chalk

Stage: Empty

Setting: MC enters stage carrying small blackboard and piece of chalk. He greets audience, and introduces the "Great Swabini."

The Performance

MC: Ladies and Gentlemen. I'm so very happy to be with you tonight, and I have the great pleasure to introduce you to one of the world's greatest mindreaders. He's here tonight to demonstrate his wonderful skill of entering your mind to reveal your thoughts. Without further ado, ladies and gentlemen, The Great Swabini.

Mindreader: *(Enters with much flourish, takes bow, and prepares to entertain.)*

MC: Now for tonight's demonstration. I have this small blackboard, and will solicit you, the members of our audience, to give me a number, UP TO FIVE, and the Great Swabini will tell us what number you have selected. Now, Mr. Great, please turn your back and we'll select the first number.

Mindreader: *(Turns with his back to the audience.)*

MC: *(To audience.)* Just hold up your fingers, UP TO FIVE, and we'll select a number and put it on this blackboard. Please don't speak out or The Great Swabini might hear you. Just hold up your fingers and we'll select a number. *(Looks over audience and selects the number THREE. Writes "3" on blackboard and shows it to entire audience, then places the blackboard on floor, face down, so that it cannot be seen.)* Now, Great Swabini, please turn around and face the music . . . er, I mean the audience. We have selected a number up to five, and now it's time for you. What can the number be? *(As MC is asks the final question, he makes very large gesture as he taps the mindreader on the shoulder three times.)*

Mindreader: *(Pauses in deep concentration.)* The number you have chosen is . . . THREE!

MC: That's exactly right. Let's hear it for The Great Swabini. *(Looks at audience as if there are doubters.)* Mr. Great, I think there are some skeptics in our audience. Perhaps we should try another number. Will you please turn around again, and we'll try it again.

Mindreader: *(Turns with back to the audience.)*

MC: Let's try it once again. *(Picks up blackboard from floor.)* I don't want any of you to doubt The Great Swabini's abilities. Please hold up your hands again and we'll select another number. *(Surveys audience for another number. This time the number FOUR is selected and written on the blackboard.)* Okay, Mr. Great Swabini. Turn back around and we'll again demonstrate your amazing abilities. We have selected another number. Please concentrate and tell us what can the number be? *(As he asks the question this time, he taps the mindreader on the shoulder four times in an exaggerated manner.)*

Mindreader: *(Pauses in deep concentration.)* The number you have chosen is FOUR!

MC: That's awesome. He's done it again. Isn't that marvelous? The Great Swabini. But wait a minute. There are still some doubters. We'll have to do it one more time so that everyone will truly believe that you are an expert. *(Picks up blackboard, erases previous number, and solicits audience. It doesn't matter how many fingers they are holding up, MC sees someone indicate the digit ZERO.)* Oh, that's great. This will really be a great test. *(Writes "0" on blackboard and places it face town on floor.)* Mr. Swabini. We are ready for another example of your amazing skill. Please turn back to face the audience and tell us the number we have selected.

Mindreader: *(Pauses for a few moments then looks at shoulder that has been tapped previously to indicate that he should be receiving taps.)*

MC: Mr. Great. We're waiting for you to tell us the number we have selected. Are you having a problem or are you a fake?

Mindreader: *(Again looks down at his shoulder, moving it to indicate that MC should be telling him the number by tapping him.)*

MC: *(To audience.)* Folks, it appears that The Great Swabini is having trouble. We'll give him just a little more time to tell us the number. Mr. Swabini, what is the number?

Mindreader: *(Looks for signal.)*

MC: C'mon you turkey. Tell us the number. *(At this point he kicks mindreader in the butt.)*

Mindreader: *(Looks surprised.)* OH . . .

MC: *(Excited)* That's right. *(Picks up blackboard to show audience.)* He got it. That is the number we've selected.

Mindreader: *(Bows)*

MC: The Amazing Great Swabini. Thank you folks. He really is a true mindreader.

Mindreader: *(Mindreader takes more bows, then both exit from stage while applause is continuing.)*

The End

ESP - MINDREADER #3

Number of Clowns: Two

Characters: The Great Krupkin, Assistant

Costumes: Turban and cape for Krupkin, regular clown wardrobe for Assistant

Props: Stool

Stage: Stool downstage center

Setting: Assistant enters stage, greets audience, and introduces The Great Krupkin.

The Performance

Assistant: Ladies and gentlemen. We have with us this evening, one of the world's greatest mentalists. A man who can identify items from the audience without even seeing them. Please welcome, The Great Krupkin.

Krupkin: *(Enters with appropriate bows.)* Good evening ladies and gentleman. I want to let you know that what you see this evening is totally unrehearsed, totally on the up and up, and is simply a matter of concentration and my mind meeting yours through the amazing process of mentalism. My assistant will pass among you and hold up various items for me to identify. I will be totally blindfolded so as not to have any indication of the item. If you're all ready, let's begin. *(Takes seat on stage, facing audience, and puts on blindfold. Assistant goes into the audience and proceeds to hold up items.)*

Assistant: *(Holds up a shoe.)* I am holding up our first item, Krupkin. Are you ready?

Krupkin: Yes. Is this from that bald-headed guy in the back?

Assistant: No, Krupkin. And your supposed to guess the item. Not the person who gave it to me.

Krupkin: Yeah, right. I'll try to get the item.

Assistant: We're taking too long on this item, Krupkin. You're going to have to STEP up the pace, or you'll make a HEEL of yourself.

Krupkin: Is it a shoe?

Assistant: Right, Krupkin. It is a shoe. That's amazing.

Krupkin: Let's continue with another one.

Assistant: *(Holds up watch.)* Okay Krupkin. I have an item from a lady in the a audience. Can you identify this item?

Krupkin: I'm thinking now. Is the lady wearing a red sweater?

Assistant: No Krupkin. You're supposed to guess what I'm holding in the air.

Krupkin: Oh, sorry. Is the lady thinking of the item as you hold it?

Assistant: Yes, she is. You'd better HURRY UP on this one. You're running out of TIME.

Krupkin: I'm beginning to get a picture.

Assistant: I hope so. Everyone is WATCHING you.

Krupkin: Is it a WATCH?

Assistant: Yes, it is. It is a watch. This is so exciting. I'm amazed every time Krupkin does this show.

Krupkin: Let's continue with another item.

Assistant: *(Holds up purse.)* Krupkin, I'm holding up another item now. Are you getting the mental image?

Krupkin: I'm trying to locate the image.

Assistant: I'm holding it in my HAND. You'll have to hurry to BAG this one.

Krupkin: Can you give me a clue?

Assistant: It won't fit in your POCKET and you can BOOK on that.

Krupkin: It's a pocketbook or a purse?

Assistant: That's right, again. Ladies and gentlemen, the Great Krupkin. Now let's try a couple more items.

Krupkin: *(Holds up pack of matches.)* I'm holding another item, Krupkin. If you don't get this one quickly, I'll have to light a FIRE under you. I hope this turns on a LIGHT in you brain.

Krupkin: Could it be a lighter or a pack of matches?

Assistant: Krupkin is right again. Now for one last item. *(Holds up handkerchief.)* Krupkin, I'm holding up our final item. Think very carefully. I wouldn't want you to BLOW this one.

Krupkin: I'm thinking very hard. This one is difficult.

Assistant: It certainly is. It's a real BUGGER.

Krupkin: *(Thinks seriously.)* It's a hankie.

Assistant: That's right. It's amazing. Krupkin, the great mentalist. Well Krupkin, the show is about over. It's time to say good-bye.

Krupkin: It's a SALE ITEM. Something at a discount.

Assistant: No, Krupkin. We're not guessing now. We're finished.

Krupkin: Finished. A piece of shiny flooring . . . furniture . . . varnish . . . ?

Assistant: No. It's time to wrap up the show.

Krupkin: Tin foil . . . wrapping paper . . . ?

Assistant: Cut it out Krupkin.

Krupkin: Scissors . . . a knife . . . a lawn mower . . ?

Assistant: No Krupkin. It's time to exit.

Krupkin: A door?

Assistant: We're leaving.

Krupkin: A rake?

Assistant: Bon Voyage.

Krupkin: An ocean liner?

Assistant: Quit, while were ahead.

Krupkin: Lettuce?

Assistant: Whoa.

Krupkin: A horse?

Assistant: Quit hamming it up.

Krupkin: A pig?

Assistant: We're done. *(Removes Krupkin's blindfold and assists Krupkin from the stage.)* You dummy.

Krupkin: Charlie McCarthy . . . ?

The End

Note: Be creative. Think of any item and then brainstorm with friends for puns to use for clues. Have fun with it. Some additional articles and clue lines are described below.

Book: If you can READ our minds on this one, it'll be a PAGE out of history.

Ring: Let's not go ROUND AND ROUND on this one. If I were a betting man, I'd bet more than a DIME ON this one.

Hat: It'll be hard to TOP this one. A correct identification will CAP off your performance.

Wig (toupee): Don't get HARRIED trying to get this one. It might be kind of RUGGED.

continued on next page

Comb: This will take a FINE TOOTHED examination. I suggest you HAIRY up and get it.

Glasses: Don't make a SPECTACLE of yourself. People will SEE right through you.

Mirror: You can REFLECT on past successes to get this one.

Keys: Don't get LOCKED in on this one. Be sure you don't bring up any SKELETONS from the past.

Perfume: Don't STINK the place up trying to get this one. It could be from Italy, like FROM-A ROME-A.

Cigarette: Holy SMOKE. I hope you don't miss this one.

Nail file: If you're brain's not working right, I'll refer you to my doctor. He's a MAN OF CURES. He has a lot of records on FILE.

Pen: Don't WRITE this one off. I have an INKLING you can get it.

Checkbook: Better CHECK your thinking on this one. I'm BANKING on you getting it.

Calendar: Make a DATE to get this one. Some of your answers are rather WEEK.

Credit card: I hope you'll DISCOVER this answer and MASTER this one. It's really INTEREST—ing.

Knife: Better CUT through the mental waves to name this one.

Hairbrush: Don't BRUSH this aside. Your friend HARRY could identify this.

HAMBURGER STAND

Number of Clowns: Two

Characters: Chef, clown (Customer)

Costumes: Regular clown wardrobe

Props: Foam hamburger, lettuce, pickle, Swiss cheese, tomato, onion rings, flat hamburger bun with footprint on one side of it, chef's apron and hat, small table, table-top with table cloth and vase attached to it

Stage: Small table near center

Setting: Customer enters empty stage.

The Performance

Customer: I can't find it. I've been looking everywhere but I can't find it. *(Looks up and sees that an audience is present.)* Oh, hello. Hey, have you seen the hamburger stand? I've been looking everywhere and I can't find it. I looked over here *(walks to one side of stage)*, and I didn't find it. I looked way over there *(goes to other side of stage)* and I didn't find it. I looked way out there *(points to the back of the audience),* and I didn't find it. I even looked over here and . . . .

Chef: *(Enters carrying small table under his arm.)*

Customer: Why, hello there. I've been looking for the hamburger stand, and I can't find it. It used to be right here. Did you see it?

Chef: Well sure. It's still right here.

Customer: Right here? It doesn't look like it did last year.

Chef: No? Well, what did it look like last year?

Customer: Well, last year it was really neat. It had a table cloth, and flowers, and all kinds of nice things.

Chef: *(Flips table-top over revealing table cloth and vase with flowers.)* Still does.

Customer: Now that's the hamburger stand I remember. *(To audience.)* Ya' know, there are two very special things I really like about this hamburger stand. The first thing is that no matter how many times you've been here, he always remembers exactly how you like your burger. Even if you've only been here one time, and come back a year later, he still remembers exactly how you like it. He never forgets.

Chef: I never forget.

Customer: And the second thing I like is if you're in a hurry, this is the place to be, because he's FAST.

Chef: I'm FAST.

Customer: Hey, would you do me a favor?

Chef: What's that? What do you want me to do?

Customer: Would you make me a hamburger?

Chef: Sure. I'd love to make you a hamburger.

Customer: Make it right away.

Chef: Sure. How do you want it?

Customer: Just like I always have it. C'mon, you

70

remember. *(To audience.)* He never forgets.

Chef: Oh yeah, I never forget.

Customer: And he's fast.

Chef: And I'm fast.

Customer: I'll tell you what. I'm going to tell them exactly how I like my hamburger while you make it. Okay?

Chef: Okay. I won't listen to you. You just tell them. *(Chef does listen to hear what Customer is saying to audience.)*

Customer: He starts off with a big old hamburger bun, about this big around. *(Shows size with his hands.)* Then he puts on that thick juicy hamburger. *(Chef puts ingredients together as Customer describes each item.)* I can hear it cooking now. He puts on that top bun, and brings it over to you . . . *(Chef brings out burger on bun and starts to hand it to Customer, but Customer continues describing)* on a nice crispy bed of lettuce. I love lettuce. That's my favorite. I love it.

Chef: *(When Chef hears about the lettuce, he stops before handing burger to Customer and quickly pulls it back.)* A nice crispy bed of what?

Customer: A bed of lettuce. Is that my hamburger?

Chef: NOOOOO! Your's has a nice crispy bed of lettuce, remember?

Customer: Yeah. Now I remember. He never forgets.

Chef: I never forget.

Customer: Amazing, and he's fast, too.

Chef: Yeah. I'm fast.

Customer: *(To audience.)* He starts off with a big ol' bun about this big around. *(Chef put ingredients together as Customer describes each item.)* Puts on that crispy bed of lettuce. Puts on that big juicy hamburger, puts it right on top and puts it on the bun. Then he brings it over to you . . . *(Chef starts to bring it out)* with a nice piece of melted Swiss cheese on it. I love Swiss cheese.

Chef: *(Realizes that burger does not have the Swiss cheese on it.)* Hey, a nice piece of melted Swiss what?

Customer: Swiss Cheese. Is that mine?

Chef: NOOOOOO! Your's has a piece of melted Swiss cheese, remember?

Customer: Ah, I remember. He never forgets.

Chef: I never forget.

Customer: And he's fast.

Chef: I'm fast. *(Hurries to back of table to work on burger.)*

Customer: Well, he starts off with a big ol' hamburger bun about this big around, puts on that nice crispy bed of lettuce, puts on the juicy burger, a nice piece of melted Swiss cheese, and puts that on the bun, (chef starts to bring it out) then he tops it off with a slice of round red tomato. Do you like red tomatoes? I love em'.

Chef: *(Brings out burger, minus tomato.)* Hey, a slice of round red what?

Customer: Red tomato. Is that mine?

Chef: *(Asking audience.)* Is this his? NOOOOOO! Your's has a nice round red tomato, remember?

Customer: Oh, yeah. Now I remember. He never forgets.

Chef: I never forget.

Customer: And he's fast.

Chef: I'm fast.

Customer: He starts off with a bun about this big around, puts on that crispy bed of lettuce, then the thick juicy hamburger. He puts on that melted Swiss cheese and then that round red tomato and the other bun . . . *(Chef brings out burger)* and tops it off with a couple of onion rings. I love onion rings.

Chef: A couple of what?

Customer: Onion rings. Is that mine?

Chef: *(To audience.)* Is this his? NOOOOOO! Your's has onion rings, remember?

Customer: I remember. He never forgets.

Chef: I never forget.

Customer: And he's fast.

Chef: I'm fast.

Customer: He starts off with a big ol' hamburger bun, puts on that crispy bed of lettuce, puts on that big juicy hamburger and the melted Swiss cheese. Then a nice piece of round red tomato, a couple of onion rings and brings it over to me . . . *(Chef brings burger)* topped off with a nice little piece of pickle.

Chef: A little piece of what?

Customer: A piece of pickle. Is that mine?

Chef: *(Exasperated, to audience.)* Is this his? NOOOOOO! Your's has a nice piece of pickle, remember?

Customer: Now I remember. He never forgets.

Chef: I never forget.

Customer: And he's fast, too.

Chef: I'm fast.

Customer: Ya' know, I'm kind of in a hurry. Would you do me a favor?

Chef: *(Shakes head agreeably, but is tired.)*

Customer: Would you put a pickle on top of that one and step on it? I'm in a hurry.

Chef: Put a pickle on the top of this one and step on it?

Customer: Yeah. He's going to put the pickle on it for me and then I'll be all set. He starts off with the big ol' hamburger bun . . .

Chef: *(Interrupts)* Hey, you want me to put a pickle on top of this one?

Customer: Put the pickle on it. . . and step on it. . . . I'm in a hurry.

Chef: Are you sure that's what you want me to do?

Customer: *(To audience.)* What did I ask him to do? *(Audience responds.)* And what do I want him to do? *(Audience responds.)* That's not so difficult, is it?

Chef: *(Puts pickle on top of burger, places it on the floor in back of table and steps on it, alternating feet)* Special orders don't upset us. *(Brings out burger bun with footprints on top of it.)*

Customer: What's that?

Chef: You told me to step on it.

Customer: I'm gonna get you.

Chef: No you won't.

Customer: I won't? Why not?

Chef: 'Cause I'm fast. *(Customer chases Chef from stage.)*

The End

PAINTERS

Number of Clowns: Two

Characters: Painter boss (Boss), assistant (Painter)

Costumes: Painter clothes, one pair of tear-away pants

Props: Two large buckets, two paint buckets, one roll wallpaper (vinyl), clipboard, four foam paint brushes, card table, chair or small ladder, paint and wallpaper paste (The paint is made from whipping soapsuds into the proper consistency and adding coloring. The wallpaper paste is the same as the soapsuds, but without the coloring.)

Stage: Two buckets with wallpaper paste, card table, chair (or ladder)

The Performance

Painter Boss enters carrying clipboard and wallpaper (rolled up under arm). He leads assistant Painter, who is carrying two buckets of paint. They walk on stage with Boss looking around surveying the situation, while Painter is skylarking. Boss suddenly stops and Painter continues walking, crashing into Boss's back. Boss drops the clipboard when he is hit.

Boss turns around, sees Painter and pushes Painter. Painter forcibly places buckets on the ground with one landing on Boss's toe. Boss slaps Painter. Painter spins around and falls. Painter gets up as Boss is reaching down to pick up clipboard. Painter kicks Boss. Boss falls forward from the kick.

Painter picks up the paint buckets and steps back. Boss takes a paintbrush from Painter's bucket and paints

Painter's shirt. Painter sets buckets down, then throws paint on Boss by flicking the brush. Boss flicks paint back on Painter, then bends down again to pick up the clipboard. Painter hits Boss on the butt with paintbrush while Boss is bent over. Boss gets up, takes brush from Painter and paints all of Painter's clothing.

Boss says, "Let's get to work." Boss takes wallpaper roll and unrolls it on table while Painter is getting paste ready. Painter takes brush with paste. As he brings brush down on the paper, Boss pulls the paper off the table. Painter misses and looks surprised. Boss puts paper back on the table. Painter tries again to put paste on paper. As Painter brings the brush down, Boss pulls paper out of the way again. Boss puts paper back on table again (third time). Painter is determined to hit it. He swings the brush at the paper as it is being removed. As he does, he misses the paper and hits Boss in the face (or chest) with the brush.

Boss is mad, but says, "Let's get this paper up. You get up on that ladder (or chair) and take this paper with you." Painter picks up a paste bucket, holding it on his shoulder, and holds the wallpaper in his other hand. While climbing onto the chair he leans backward and spills the paint back onto Boss, behind him.

Painter comes down from chair, laughs and checks out the wallpaper. Boss gets another bucket of paste and puts it on Painter's head. Painter spins around, getting wrapped up in the paper. Boss spins him back around by pulling on the paper.

Boss says, "Now, let's get this painting done." Boss goes across stage, picks up one of the buckets of paint and begins to pretend he is painting a wall. Painter comes up behind and pulls Boss by the belt indicating that painting should begin on the other side of the stage. Annoyed, Boss slaps Painter's hand from the belt and continues trying to paint his side of the stage. Painter comes up behind Boss again and pulls on his belt. Boss, more annoyed, again removes Painter's hand from the belt, and tells him to "go over there and paint." Painter starts to cross the stage but changes his mind. Again he tugs on Boss's belt to try to get Boss to join him on the other side of the stage.

Boss is really annoyed and tells Painter to go away. Painter, finally accepting the fact that Boss will not help, waves at Boss and crosses the stage to begin painting on the other side. Boss calls to Painter to "come over here and paint." Painter motions that Boss should "get lost" and returns to painting his wall. Boss crosses stage, and plans to pull Painter's pants to tug him across the stage to help. When Boss tugs on Painter's pants, they break away, and Painter is left standing there in his underwear. Painter notices his situation, looks around to see Boss holding the pants, and chases Boss from the stage.

The End

Note: Tear-away pants are made by ripping out the seams from a pair of pants and sewing Velcro on both edges of the seams. The Velcro holds the outside edge of pant legs together, when pants are pulled, the Velcro releases and pants are torn free.

THE PICKPOCKET

Number of Clowns: Two

Characters: Pickpocket, Stooge (planted in audience)

Costumes: Regular clown wardrobe

Props: Cloth bag to fit over hands, three-foot piece of rope, comedy underwear, wallet, wristwatch

Stage: Empty

Setting: Clown is introduced as the "World's Greatest Pickpocket." He enters the stage with a lot of flair, accepting applause from audience.

The Performance

Pickpocket: Thank you, thank you. I am the world's greatest pickpocket and to prove it, I'll present an exhibition right here. In fact, I'll pick the pocket of someone from the audience. Is there someone out there who would like to volunteer?

Stooge: *(Volunteers to help and is invited to come up on the stage.)*

Pickpocket: Thank you for volunteering to assist me tonight. What is your name?

Stooge: My name is _____.

Pickpocket: Well _____, have we ever met before?

Stooge: No, I've never met you.

Pickpocket: Then how do you know it's me? Ha, ha, just kidding. We have never seen each other, but tonight

79

_____, you are going to be amazed. Have you ever had your pocket picked before?

Stooge: No, and I don't think you're going to do it tonight, either.

Pickpocket: *(Holds up watch, on the side opposite of where Stooge is standing.)* Well, perhaps not. By the way, can you tell me what time it is?

Stooge: *(Looks at wrist and discovers watch is missing. Looks around and sees that Pickpocket is holding it.)* Hey, that's my watch. How did you get it?

Pickpocket: I told you I am the world's greatest pickpocket.

Stooge: Well that was just lucky. Are you through with me now?

Pickpocket: *(Holds up a wallet.)* Yes, you can return to your seat now. *(Stooge begins to leave.)* But first, can you loan me a buck?

Stooge: *(Reaches for his wallet and discovers it missing. Looks at Pickpocket, and sees it in his hand.)* Hey, that's my wallet. How did you get it?

Pickpocket: I knew it was yours. There was nothing in it.

Stooge: Well, I've got something that will prevent you from ever picking another pocket. I've got the special Pickpocket Preventer.

Pickpocket: You've got what?

Stooge: I knew you were going to be here, and I invented the Pickpocket Preventer.

Pickpocket: Nothing can prevent me from picking pockets. Bring it out and let me show you it won't work.

Stooge: *(Gets cloth bag.)* Here it is. This will stop you for good.

Pickpocket: It's just a bag. How's that going to stop me?

Stooge: Well, just put your hands together in front of you. *(Pickpocket puts hands together and Stooge puts bag over hands. He then ties rope around the bag and wrists of Pickpocket.)* Now, that will stop you for good. You can't pick my pocket now.

Pickpocket: This will never stop me. Watch. *(Waves bag at Stooge and utters some magic incantations.)* There. Now I've picked your pocket again.

Stooge: You haven't done anything. You just waved your hands and said some stupid stuff. You haven't done anything.

Pickpocket: Yeah? Well, I picked your pocket. Here, I'll do it again. *(Waves hands again and utters magic words.)*

Stooge: You haven't done anything. You're a fake.

Pickpocket: Well, if you don't believe me, then untie this thing and I'll show you.

Stooge: I'll prove it to you and everyone here in the audience. *(Unties hands and removes bag.)*

Pickpocket: *(Stands there holding some clown underwear.)* See, you didn't stop me.

Stooge: *(Look under his belt and pretends to discover underwear is missing.)* Get out of here. *(Stooge chases Pickpocket off stage.)*

The End

Acknowledgement: This gag was first shown to me by Earl "Mr. Clown" Chaney at a clown seminar in Chicago. It is an old gag, and I'm grateful to Mr. Clown for showing it.

RING-RING

Number of Clowns: Two (can also be performed by three clowns, see Option 2 on page 87)

Characters: Clown A, Clown B

Costumes: Regular clown wardrobe

Props: Long rubber bicycle inner tube or long string of pencil balloons

Stage: Empty

Setting: Clown A enters stage with Clown B. Clown A is carrying an inner tube (or string of pencil balloons). They are talking about Clown A's new invention—the ultra-supersonic long-distance telephone.

The Performance

Clown A: Hey _____, let me show you my new invention. It will let you talk to your friends all over the world.

Clown B: Really? How does it work?

Clown A: Well it's really very simple. You hold one end of this telephone equipment *(the inner tube)* and I'll hold the other end. I say, "Ring-ring," and you say, "Hello." Then I say, "I have a telephone call for _____," and you say, "Let me have it." Then I'll let you have it. Doesn't that sound like fun.

Clown B: It sure does.

Clown A: Now you stand right here and I'll go over there and talk to you. *(Clown A positions Clown B, turns his back and takes a few steps across the stage. When*

Clown A begins to move, Clown B takes the identical steps and follows him like a shadow. When Clown A gets to his spot he turns around) Hey, I thought I told you to stay over there.

Clown B: *(Points to floor next to Clown A.)* No, you said to stand right here.

Clown A: *(Takes Clown B back to original spot.)* Now, I want you so stand right HERE. Do you understand?

Clown B: Sure. I'm supposed to stand right HERE.

Clown A: Okay. Now I'm going over there. *(Clown A turns and again walks across the stage with Clown B following him. When Clown A gets to other end and turns around, Clown B moves in back of him so that Clown A doesn't see him. Clown A is bewildered, he can't figure out what happened to Clown B. As Clown A turns back, B again moves so A can't see him. Finally A makes a quick turn and discovers Clown B.)*

Clown A: What are you doing here? I told you to stand over THERE.

Clown B: No you didn't. You told me to stand right HERE and I'm standing HERE.

Clown A: Well I meant for you to stand over THERE.

Clown B: You didn't say that. If that's what you meant, why didn't you say that?

Clown A: You know what I meant. Now get over there. *(He again takes Clown B back to the original spot. When they get there, Clown A takes out a piece of* *paper and places it on the floor.)* Now, I want you to stand right on this piece of paper and don't move.

Clown B: Okay. I'll stand right on the paper.

Clown A: *(Turns and walks across the stage.)*

Clown B: *(Quickly picks up the paper, follows Clown A across the stage, places the paper on the floor, and quickly stands on it)*

Clown A: *(Turns around. Is disturbed to find Clown B standing next to him again.)* I told you to stand on the paper. Now what are you doing over here?

Clown B: I'm standing on the paper. See?

Clown A: That's enough. Do you want to see this telephone or not?

Clown B: Sure. I thought you were showing it to me.

Clown A: Well, take your paper and get over there where I showed you.

Clown B: *(Picks up paper and moves back to his original spot.)*

Clown A: Ring-ring.

Clown B: Hello, Mario's Pizza Place, what would you like?

Clown A: No! You don't remember anything. *(Walks across the stage and stands next to Clown B.)* Let me tell you again. I say, "Ring-ring." You say, "Hello." I say, "I have a call for _____." You say, "Let me have it." Do you understand?

Clown B: I think I have it now.

Clown A: Okay, let's try again. *(He walks across stage.)* Ring-ring.

Clown B: You have reached _____ answering machine. _____ isn't here right now. Please leave your message at the beep.

Clown A: No! No! *(Walks over to Clown B again.)* I say, "Ring-ring." You say, "Hello." I say, "I have a call for _____." You say, "Let me have it." Can you remember that?

Clown B: Sure. What do you think I am, stupid? *(Clown A gives a look to the audience.)* Let's see. You say, "Ring-ring." I say, "Hello." You say, you have a call for _____. I say, "Let me have it." I think I'm ready.

Clown A: Ring-ring.

Clown B: Hello.

Clown A: *(Appears relieved that clown B is finally catching on.)* I have a call for _____. *(No response from Clown B. He seems to be trying to remember his line.)*

Clown B: *(Whispers across stage.)* I can't remember what to say.

Clown A: Let me have it. Let me have it! LET ME

HAVE IT!

Clown B: (Lets go of his end of the inner tube, which snaps Clown A in the stomach. Clown A is very mad and chases Clown B off the stage).

The End

OPTION 1 : Rather than use an inner tube, you could use another prop. I recently saw this skit done with a garden hose instead of the inner tube. While Clown B was responding, Clown A was loading water into the hose. When B said, "Let me have it" Clown A blew into the hose spraying Clown B with the water.

OPTION 2: A third clown (Clown C) can be used. The third clown would appear as follows: Clown B has just been sprayed with the water.

Clown B: Hey. I'm all wet. I don't like this telephone at all.

Clown A: Now, now, you're just upset because I tricked you. Wouldn't you like to pull the same trick on someone else?

Clown B: *(Clown B's eyes light up as he thinks about getting another clown.)* Yeah, but who would we get? *(Clown C wanders onto the stage. They both look at Clown C and then at each other realizing that here is their victim.)*

Clown B: Hey _____. Would you like to see _____ new invention? It's called a telephone. *(Clown A is waiting to participate.)*

Clown C: Sure. I like inventions. How does it work?

Clown B: Well, I'll let _____ explain how it works. *(Clown A explains the system, just as he did for Clown B, but without the walking. Clown C appears to understand, and A hands him the end of the hose.)*

Clown A: Ring-ring.

Clown C: Hello. *(Clown C folds the hose in half and holds it so that no water can come out of it.)*

Clown A: I have a call for _____.

Clown C: Let me have it.

Clown A: *(Blows into the hose, but nothing happens. Clown A looks at Clown B and tries blowing into the hose again, with no results. Clown C is looking at hose and notices that it is not working.)*

Clown C: *(To Clown B.)* It isn't working. Do you think you can fix it?

Clown B: Sure. I can fix it. *(Clown C hands end of hose to Clown B.)*

Clown A: *(Blows into the hose and gets Clown B all wet again. Clown B is upset, and a chase-off ensues.)*

The End

STAGECOACH

Number of Clowns: Two

Characters: Two cowboys (Stagecoach Driver and Shotgun)

Costumes: Western garb

Props: Two chairs, shotgun, mail bag, whip for Driver

Stage: Two chairs in center of downstage

Setting: The Stagecoach Driver and Shotgun enter the stage and walk over to chairs.

The Performance

Driver: *(To Shotgun.)* Have a seat on the old stagecoach. We've gotta ride and take the mail to Denver. *(They both take seats, Shotgun to the Driver's right. Driver appears to hold reins as if controlling the horses. Driver shouts for horses to begin, cracks his whip, and begins bouncing and weaving as if riding on a stagecoach. Shotgun sits still. Driver notices that Shotgun is not bouncing, looks at him, and gives him a jab to the ribs. Shotgun begins to bounce, too.)*

Shotgun: *(Looks back behind them and appears concerned about something.)* Hey, boss. There's someone riding real fast toward us. I think this means trouble.

Driver: How big is he?

Shotgun: *(Holds thumb and index finger about three inches apart)* He's about this big.

Driver: No problem. He's about three days behind us. Keep on riding. *(They ride for awhile)*

Shotgun: *(Looks back again.)* He's gaining on us.

Driver: How big is he now?

Shotgun: *(Indicating with both hands about eight inches.)* He's this big.

Driver: No problem. He's two days behind us. Keep on riding. *(The ride some more.)*

Shotgun: *(Looks back again and gets excited.)* He's really gaining on us! He's almost caught up with us.

Driver: How big is he now?

Shotgun: *(Indicates that person is about 18 inches tall).*

Driver: No problem. He's still a day behind us. *(The ride some more.)*

Shotgun: *(Looks back again and is now very worried.)* He's almost here! What are we gonna' do?

Driver: How big is he now?

Shotgun: He's about this big. *(Indicates about three feet tall.)*

Driver: That looks like trouble. Shoot him.

Shotgun: What?

Driver: I said shoot him.

Shotgun: *(Hesitant)* I can't. I can't shoot him.

Driver: Why not?

Shotgun: *(Indicating with thumb and index finger)* I've known him since he was this big.

Driver: Well, if you're not going to shoot him then you may as well join him. *(Driver pushes Shotgun off of chair and onto the ground. Shotgun gets up and chases Driver off the stage.)*

The End

STARGAZER

Number of Clowns: Two

Characters: Astronomer (Stargazer), Stooge

Costumes: Normal clown wardrobe, but Stargazer wears cape, dunce cap, etc.

Props: Telescope, small stool, Venus (doll without arms), Pluto (Disney dog), star, giant Milky Way bar, big Comet (cleanser) can with Haley written on back of it, thermometer, small pan or ladle (Little Dipper), bigger pan or ladle (Big Dipper), sponge hammer

Stage: Telescope and small stool in center of stage

Setting: Stargazer is on stage with telescope. Sign says "See the Stars only 25 cents." Stooge enters, looks at sign, and talks to astronomer.

The Performance

Stooge: Hey, can you really see the stars through that thing?

Stargazer: Sure. You can see the stars, the moon, comets, and all the heavenly bodies.

Stooge: I'd like to see Miss Universe, she has a heavenly body.

Stargazer: That's not what I mean. I'm talking celestial stuff. Give me a quarter and I'll let you have a look.

Stooge: Okay. Sounds good. I'd like to see a star.

Stargazer: *(Brings out a large star on a stick, and holds it in front of telescope.)* Do you see that?

Stooge: Yeah. That's some star, but don't you have any more? I want to see a lot of stars.

Stargazer: *(Holds up huge Milky Way bar.)* How's this? It's the Milky Way.

Stooge: WOW! I never thought I'd see that many stars. The Milky Way . . .

Stargazer: *(Holds up big can of Comet).* Look again. I think there's a comet passing by.

Stooge: Hey, you're right. I do see a comet.

Stargazer: *(Turns can around to show the word "Haley" on back.)*

Stooge: I think it's Haley's comet. But I want to see a lot of stars.

Stargazer: Okay. Just wait a minute. Would you like to see some planets?

Stooge: *(Looks away from scope, and asks Stargazer.)* Can I really see planets through this thing? Can I see Venus? I heard it's out there.

Stargazer: (Holds up doll without arms) Sure. Just look a little to the left. Can you see Venus?

Stooge: Yes I see Venus. Can I see Mercury?

Stargazer: Sure. Just look through it again. I think you'll see Mercury. *(Holds up a thermometer.)*

Stooge: You're right. I think I do see Mercury. Can I see far enough to see Pluto?

Stargazer: Sure. Just turn it a bit to the right. *(Holds up Pluto doll.)* Would you like to see the Big Dipper? *(Holds up big dipper.)*

Stooge: I see it now. The Big Dipper. Isn't the Little Dipper right near it?

Stargazer: Sure, just look a little bit to your left. *(Holds up Little Dipper.)*

Stooge: There it is, but I want to see lots of stars. Can't I see lots of stars?

Stargazer: Sure. You can see LOTS of stars. *(Hits Stooge on the head with a sponge hammer)*

Stooge: *(Falls off of the stool and rolls around dazed.)* I see lots of stars now. Hey, you hit me with a hammer. That's not fair. *(Gets up and chases Stargazer off the stage.)*

The End

TALKING MACHINE

Number of Clowns: Two

Characters: Talking Machine, Clown

Costumes: Robot-type for machine, regular clown wardrobe for Clown

Props: Money receiving box (hanging around neck of the Talking Machine)

Stage: Empty

Setting: Talking Machine is wheeled onto stage on hand truck by stagehand. (Note: Hand truck can also be wheeled onto stage by a third clown wearing coveralls.) Talking Machine is placed in standing position at downstage center. Clown enters and sees Talking Machine. Clown is curious about this machine and looks around it to see what it does. All dialogue in this skit is for Talking Machine, although the Clown can insert appropriate comments as he feels appropriate. The more reactions and comments from the Clown, the better this skit presentation is for the audience. Imagine yourself discovering a machine and getting ripped-off every time you insert a coin. You would be rather upset, too.

The Performance

Clown: *(Takes out coin and inserts in into box in front of Talking Machine.)*

Talking Machine: *(Standing with head down. After coin is inserted, head comes up and machine starts talking in robot-like voice.)* Hello. I am your friendly talking machine. I am here to help you. *(Machine drops head because time/money has run out.)*

Clown: *(Inserts another coin.)*

Talking Machine: *(Raises head)* Hello. I am your friendly talking machine. I am here to help you. Would you like to know how I can help you? *(Drops head)*

Clown: *(Annoyed, but deposits another coin)*

Talking Machine: *(Raises head.)* Hello. I am your friendly talking machine. I am here to help you. Would you like to know how I can help you? You are sad and lonely. *(Drops head.)*

Clown: *(Deposit another coin.)*

Talking Machine: *(Raises head.)* Hello. I am your friendly talking machine. I am here to help you. Would you like to know how I can help you? You are sad and lonely. Would you like to know how not to be sad and lonely? *(Drops head.)*

Clown: *(Deposits another coin.)*

Talking Machine: *(Raises head.)* Hello. I am your friendly talking machine. I am here to help you. Would you like to know how I can help you? You are sad and lonely. Would you like to know how not to be sad and lonely? You need a friend *(Drops head.)*

Clown: *(Deposits another coin.)*

Talking Machine: *(Raises head.)* Hello. I am your friendly talking machine. I am here to help you. Would you like to know how I can help you? You are sad and lonely. Would you like to know how not to be sad and lonely? You need a friend. Would you like to know how to find a friend? *(Drops head.)*

Clown: *(Deposits another coin.)*

Talking Machine: *(Raises head.)* Hello. I am your friendly talking machine. I am here to help you. Would you like to know how I can help you? You are sad and lonely. Would you like to know how not to be sad and lonely? You need a friend. Would you like to know how to find a friend? You give them lots of money—friend. *(Talking Machine comes to life, revealing what was really happening.)*

Clown: Hey you! You cheated me. *(Clown chases Talking Machine off.)*

The End

Acknowledgement: I first saw this skit performed by Brenda Marshall and Linda Hulet.

TELESCOPE

Number of Clowns: Two

Characters: Astronomer, Stooge

Costumes: Regular clown wardrobe, but Astronomer wears cape, dunce cap, etc.

Props: Telescope, small stool, star on a stick, giant Milky Way bar, large can of Comet cleanser with the word "Haley" written on the back, spark-ring or sparkler, bucket of water. (Telescope is constructed of PVC material. It is about 5 - 6 feet long and has a fitting on the eyepiece side. This fitting has a screw-on cap to prevent the water from coming out the first time it is poured into scope. Cap must be able to be unscrewed to allow water to flow through later in the skit. Fitting can be made from the top of an ordinary plastic bottle.)

Stage: Telescope and small stool in center of stage

Setting: This skit is a variation the Stargazer skit described earlier. Astronomer is on stage with a telescope. Sign says "See the Stars only 25 cents." Stooge enters, looks at the sign and approaches to astronomer.

The Performance

Stooge: Hey. Can you really see the stars through that thing?

Astronomer: Sure. You can see the stars, the moon, comets, and all the heavenly bodies.

Stooge: I'd like to see Miss Universe, she has a heavenly body.

Astronomer: That's not what I mean. I'm talking

celestial stuff. Give me a quarter and I'll let you have a look.

Stooge: Okay. Sounds good. I'd like to see a star. (Gives money to Astronomer.)

Astronomer: *(Brings out large star on a stick, and holds it in front of the telescope.)* Do you see that?

Stooge: Yeah. That's some star, but don't you have any more? I want to see a lot of stars.

Astronomer: *(Holds up huge Milky Way bar.)* How's this? It's the Milky Way.

Stooge: WOW! I never thought I'd see that many stars. The Milky Way. . .

Astronomer: *(Holds up a big can of Comet.)* Look again. I think there's a comet passing by.

Stooge: Hey, you're right. I do see a comet.

Astronomer: *(Turns can around to reveal the word "Haley" on back.)*

Stooge: I think it's Haley's comet.

Astronomer: Probably so. You'd better look some more. I think it's getting cloudy. Maybe there's a storm coming up. There's lightening in the air. *(Shoots off funken-spark ring or lights sparkler.)*

Stooge: Hey, I just saw the lightening. Do you think it's going to rain?

Astronomer: I think it is. If you look through the telescope, you'll be the first one to see the rain.

Stooge: Oh good. I want to see the rain first.

Astronomer: You will *(Pours water into telescope and waits to see Stooge get wet.)*

Stooge: I don't see any rain. Are you sure it's raining?

Astronomer: It sure is. Maybe it takes a while for you to see it. *(Pours more water in and looks to see Stooge get wet.)*

Stooge: I think this is a fake. It isn't working. You'd better check it.

Astronomer: Okay. I'll check it. *(Tips big end of scope down and gets hit in face with water)*

Stooge: Is it working better now?

Astronomer: *(Drying off.)* This end is okay. Let me check that end.

Stooge: Okay. We can switch places. *(They change places.)*

Astronomer: *(Sits down on stool.)* I'd better adjust the focus on this scope *(Unscrews cap off end of PVC scope.)*

Stooge: Do you see rain yet?

Astronomer: Not yet. I'd better check the focus.

Stooge: It's beginning to rain more now. *(Pours water into top of scope. It goes through to soak Astronomer.)*

Astronomer: Hey, there's nothing wrong with this. I can feel the rain now.

Stooge: I know. I saw another one of these telescopes down the street.

Astronomer: Why you. I oughtta . . . *(Chase off.)*

The End

THROW AWAY GARBAGE CAN

Number of Clowns: Two

Characters: Garbage Collector, Clown

Costumes: Overalls for Garbage Collector, normal clown wardrobe for Clown

Props: Large garbage collection container, small broken garbage can, some additional garbage to be picked up

Stage: Garbage can on stage

Setting: Garbage Collector crosses stage with large garbage container. Sees garbage on stage. Empties it into his container and moves across stage. Clown comes on to stage carrying broken garbage can containing some small garbage.

The Performance

Clown: Well, I see the garbage collector has already come by. I'll just place this broken garbage can here for him to take the next time. *(Places garbage can on stage and leaves.)*

Garbage Collector: *(Enters and sees small broken garbage can. Picks it up. Empties contents into his large garbage container, replaces small garbage can back on stage, and leaves.)*

Clown: *(Comes out. Sees small garbage can still on stage, but empty.)* Hmm. I guess he didn't know he was supposed to take this can, too. I'll smash it up some more so he'll know he is supposed to take it.

Garbage Collector: *(Walks by. Sees small broken garbage can. Picks it up. Empties contents into his large garbage container, replaces small garbage can back on stage, and leaves.)*

Clown: *(Comes back out. Sees can again. Begins to get upset that garbage collector has not taken can.)* What! He still didn't take it? I'll just put a nice note on it, then maybe he'll do it right. *(Gets paper, marking pen, and masking tape. Makes sign that says, "TAKE THIS" and tapes it onto the can, then leaves.)*

Garbage Collector: *(Walks by. Sees small broken garbage can. Takes sign from garbage can, replaces can, and leaves)*

Clown: *(Returns. Sees that can is still there but note is gone. He gets very upset and takes can off stage. He keeps watching for Garbage Collector to come by. When he sees him, he comes running onto the stage carrying the small can, shouting)* Hey! Am I too late for the garbage?

Garbage Collector: No. You're just in time. Jump in.

Clown: Great. *(He runs to large garbage container carrying small garbage can and jumps into large garbage container. Garbage Collector pushes large container from stage, with Clown in the container.)*

The End

TIDE · ALL · CHEER

Number of Clowns: Two

Characters: Ringmaster (or announcer) and Clown

Costumes: Regular clown wardrobe

Props: Large paper bag, two ropes, empty boxes of Tide, All, and Cheer

Stage: Empty

The Performance ━━━━━━━━━━━━━━━━━

Clown enters carrying a bag containing the empty soap boxes. He also has two ropes in his hand. Clown announces that he will toss the two ropes into the bag and they will come out "Tied." Ringmaster doubts that Clown can do this trick, and says so.

Undaunted, the Clown puts the bag down, takes the two ropes and spins them in his hand over his head. Then with great flourish, tosses them into the bag. He does some magic incantations over the bag and reaches in. He grabs the end of one rope and pulls it out to show them tied together, but only the one rope comes out. Surprised, he looks into the bag and pulls out the other rope.

He admits that it didn't work that time, but he will try the trick again.

Clown again spins the ropes around and tosses them into the bag. This time he does even more gestures to get the trick to work uttering some really bizarre magic words. He looks into the bag, says some more magic words and movements. Then, with great assurance, he reaches into the bag and pulls out both ropes. He holds the end of one of them into the air and lets go. The other rope falls to the ground. He is dumbfounded (a good word for a clown).

He admits that this always works the third time, so he will try again.

He twirls the ropes and tosses them into the bag. After a great deal of magic moves and words, he looks into the bag looks up with a bright grin and lets everyone know that it worked.

Ringmaster says he should show his success to the audience. With great reluctance, the Clown reaches into the bag and pulls out the empty TIDE box. "See, they are tied."

Ringmaster criticizes him and asks if that is ALL?

Clown again reaches into bag and pulls out the box of ALL, saying, "No, this is ALL."

Again Ringmaster says Clown is not really a magician and that the audience should not clap or cheer for his trick. Clown says he doesn't need it.

He reaches into bag and pulls out the next box (CHEER). "See. I brought along my own CHEER."

Clown exits amidst many groans.

The End

TUG ROPE

Number of Clowns: Two, plus off-stage assistant

Characters: Clown A, Clown B, off-stage assistant

Costumes: Normal Clown wardrobe

Props: Long rope (about 50 feet)

Stage: Empty, but must have two wing curtains and a backdrop curtain

The Performance

Clown A enters holding one end of a long rope as if dragging it across stage. Clown A gets about one-half way across stage and rope appears to be stuck. (Off-stage assistant is holding the rope.) Clown A can't pull it any farther. Clown A tries a couple of times to pull rope, each time without success. He says, "I need some help."

Clown B enters. Clown A drops the rope. Clown B picks it up and tries to pull it across the stage, without success. He tries a couple of times, but each time gets stopped since the rope won't go any further. He backs up a couple of steps, gets running start with the rope, but falls forward when the rope stops.

Clown B starts pulling rope slowly, each time getting a little farther until he disappears beyond the wings of the stage. At this point the rope runs totally across the stage, spanning it from curtain to curtain, with no clowns on stage. (Offstage assistants on each side keep rope tight and waving.)

Clown B quickly runs behind the back curtain of the stage and takes a hold on the opposite end with assistant now pulling the end where Clown B disappeared. As rope continues to be pulled across the stage, Clown B appears on the tail end of the rope, giving the appearance that he is being pulled across the stage.

The End

Note: This skit can be done with only one clown and two offstage assistants, by eliminating the first clown with the trouble. This skit can begin where Clown B enters the stage.

TWO ON A CHAIR

Number of Clowns: Two

Characters: Clown A, Clown B

Costumes: Regular clown wardrobe

Props: Two kazoos, straight-back chair

Stage: Chair in center of stage

Setting: Clown A enters carrying kazoo (or actual instrument). He nods to audience, and indicates (either verbally or in mime) that he is going to play a tune. He then sits on the chair with his legs together and plays a tune. While Clown A is playing, Clown B enters and creates the impression that he, too, will play a song. He does not see Clown A sitting on the chair. Clown B moves toward the chair (while looking at the audience), and sits on Clown A's lap. Clown B's legs are on the outside of clown A's legs. Clown B immediately is aware that something is wrong. He looks down counts the number of legs: 1-2-3-4. Both clowns jump up, and look around rather confused.

The Performance

Clown A: What do you want?

Clown B: I want to play a song.

Clown A: But there's only one chair. You can't play.

Clown B: But, I want to play, too.

Clown A: *(Pauses to think, gets an idea.)* Okay, I'll fix it so we can both play. *(Goes back upstage and tips the chair forward so it is face down.)*

Clown B: *(Excited, looks to audience.)* OH BOY! He's going to let me play too. We're going to play a duet, both of us.

Clown A: *(Returns to the front of the stage and looks at Clown B.)* Have a seat. *(Sits down on the leg part of the chair.)*

Clown B: *(Keeps his eyes on the audience, so as to create the impression that he does not see that the chair has been turned on it's side. He sits over the unsupported back of the chair.)*

Clowns A and B: *(They play the "Billboard March" or a similar fast tune. At the end of the song, Clown A jumps up and runs to the front of the stage for a bow, while Clown B falls to the floor.)*

Clown A: *(Excited about how he fooled Clown B, runs back and forth near the front of the stage)* I got him that time. He fell right on the floor. Did you see that?

Clown B: *(Standing behind Clown A, he turns the chair around 180 degrees, so that Clown A will now be sitting on the unsupported back of the chair. He invites him to join him in another song.)* Let's play a slow song this time.

Clown A: *(Does not notice that the chair has been turned around.)*

Clowns A and B: *(They both take seats with Clown B sitting on the leg part of the chair, and Clown A sitting on the unsupported back. While they play the slow tune, both get up together, shoulder-to-shoulder, slowly, to the surprise of the audience, which is expecting Clown B to get up and Clown A to fall to the floor. After thy slowly rise together, they both sit back down slowly, still playing. They then both get up again, together, and both sit down again. At the end of the song, both jump up at the* *same time, and go to the front of the stage for applause. The chair did not tip during the song.)*

Note: It is important to practice standing up together and sitting down together. If the two clowns are touching each other when sitting, one clown can indicate the rise by nudging the other slightly with his elbow.

Clown A: *(Returns to the chair and turns it back to the first position, so Clown B will be sitting on the unsupported back)*

Clown B: *(Stays in front of the stage accepting applause.)*

Clown A: *(Returns to the front of the stage.)* Let's play the fast song again.

Clown B: Okay. That was a fun song.

Clowns A and B: *(They both take seats as in the first song. Clown B does not notice that the chair has been turned back to the original position, and that he will again be sitting on the back of the chair. They again play the fast song. At the end, Clown A jumps up and Clown B falls to the floor.)*

Clown A: *(Overjoyed at fooling Clown B, he returns to the front of the stage and talks to the audience.)* I got him again. Did you see that? He fell for it again. Ha. Ha. Ha. *(He looks behind him to see that Clown B is picking the chair up over his head and is coming toward him to hit him. They run from one side of the stage to the other, then off the stage.)*

The End

THREE

CLOWNS

BALLOON CHASE

Number of Clowns: Three minimum, although four or more is better

Characters: Balloon Seller (Clown A), two or more other clowns all of which are slient except for Clown B

Costumes: Normal clown wardrobe

Props: 10 or more balloons on sticks

Stage: Empty

Setting: Balloon Seller enters arena, audience, or general performing area disrupting the show that is taking place, and talking very loudly.

The Performance

Clown A: Balloons for sale . . . balloons for sale. *(Other clowns look at Clown A, and appear to be wondering what is going on.)*

Clown B: Hey, you can't sell balloons in here. We have a show going on.

Clown A: *(Balloon seller looks quizzingly.)* I Can. Balloons for sale . . . balloons for sale.

Clown B: Listen, you can't sell balloons in here. We're doing a show and we do not sell balloons in our show.

Clown A: *(Again Balloon Seller looks perplexed and continues.)* I Can. Balloons for sale . . . balloons for sale.

Clown B: *(Asks another clown to escort balloon seller from audience. Clown and Seller appear to head for an*

exit. Clown thinks Seller is leaving and turns around to come back into the auditorium. When clown is gone, the Seller turns around and comes back.)

Clown A: Balloons for sale . . . balloons for sale . . . . Only one dollar.

Clown B: *(Again asks another clown to get rid of Balloon Seller. This time as clown approaches Seller, instead of helping Seller to the door, Clown steals the entire bunch of balloons. This initiates a balloon chase with both clowns running back and forth across the stage. As the clown is being chased by the Seller, he hands the balloons to another clown, who runs off. The balloons are handed off to other clowns on the stage and the chase continues. Meanwhile, Balloon Seller is chasing whichever clown has the balloons, in an effort to get his balloons back. The last clown running with the balloons trips and falls on them, breaking as many as possible.)*

Clown A: *(Balloon Seller gathers remainder of balloons and sticks and leaves area somewhat dejected.)*

The End

Acknowledgement: This balloon chase has been presented, for as long as I can remember, by the Moslem Temple Shrine Clowns, in Detroit, as an opener to their annual Shrine Circus. George, the balloon man, has played that part for many, many years. It was originally created by clown legend Otto Griebling.

115

THE BOX

Number of Clowns: Three

Characters: Game Hustler (Clown A), Stooge (Clown B), Clown in the Box (Clown C)

Costumes: Regular clown wardrobe

Props: Large box on wheels, three painted buckets, foam hammer, phone money

Stage: Empty

The Performance ▬▬▬▬▬▬▬▬▬▬▬▬▬▬▬

This skit is based on the old shell game. Clown A enters, pushing the box with three buckets inside. (Buckets are painted red, yellow, and blue.) Clown A takes the buckets out of the box and places each one over a hole in the top of the box. Clown A then explains to the audience that he has invented this new money-making game, and now all he has to do is find an unsuspecting customer.

At this point Clown B enters. He is stopped by Clown A and asked if he would like to win some money by playing a guessing game. Clown B agrees.

Clown A explains the game to Clown B by showing him there is nothing under two buckets (number 2 and 3 positions), but when he lifts the outside bucket (position 1), there is a clown head underneath (Clown C). Clown C just looks dumb and smiles, but does not move. Clown A explains that he will put the buckets back in their positions, and then move them around. All Clown B has to do to win the money is to identify which bucket Clown C is under.

116

Clown B agrees, and gives some money, perhaps a giant dollar bill, to Clown A. Clown A shuffles the buckets around (like in the shell game), being sure that he does not put the same colored bucket over the next hole where Clown C will appear.

Note: It is best to have each bucket painted a different color. If Clown C was under the YELLOW bucket to begin with, be sure he is under a DIFFERENT colored bucket for his second appearance, otherwise the game would be too easy. It is also recommended to have a pre-set arrangement for the appearance of Clown C. I recommend something like position 2 the first time, position 3 the second appearance, and position 1 for the third appearance.

After taking the money and switching the buckets around, Clown A asks Clown B to pick one. Clown B chooses the same color bucket that previously contained Clown C. Clown A asks the audience where they think Clown C is. Clown A says something like "How many think he is under the Blue Bucket?" Then he shows the blue bucket to be empty. "How many think he is under the Yellow Bucket?" He shows the empty yellow bucket. Then he shows that Clown C is really under the Red bucket, and in position 2.

Clown B is surprised and wants to try again. Clown A agrees, puts the buckets back in place, and collects another dollar. Clown A moves the buckets around, and then proceeds to ask the same questions, as before. Clown B guesses the same color that he last saw C under. Clown A asks the audience for their opinions again, shows the empty buckets, then reveals Clown C under the bucket in position 3.

Clown B wants to try again. Clown A takes his money and again shuffles the buckets around. When Clown A reveals Clown C this time, in position 1, he is so proud of himself that he goes to the front of the stage (in front of the box) and explains to the audience that he is so good, no one could ever outfox him and win the money. While he is doing this, Clown B, who is standing next to the clown head, takes a foam hammer from inside the box and beats the clown head down into the box. (Clown C ducks back down as he is being hit). When Clown A turns around, he is surprised, and baffled as to where Clown C went. A looks under the buckets, but can't find C, and finally pushes the box off stage laughing, having outfoxed Clown B.

The End

Alternate Ending 1: When the box is pushed off the stage, Clown C has come out of the box and is revealed sitting on the stage in back of the box. When Clown C realizes that the audience can now see him, he gets up, embarrassed, and runs off the stage following the box and Clown A.

Alternate Ending 2: After replacing all of the buckets, and not finding Clown C, Clown A is bewildered. Suddenly one of the buckets begin to move around. Clown A is surprised, and happy. He has now solved his problem and knows where Clown C has been hiding. Clown A removes the bucket but nothing is there. He bends forward and looks into the hole. At this point Clown C, inside the box, squirts Clown A with a seltzer bottle. Clown A is both embarrassed and mad, as he hurriedly pushes the box off the stage.

Note: This skit is also effective as a parade skit. One clown pushes the box while another clown is inside. The clown behind the box (pusher), lifts the buckets and shows clown head to the audience. He tries to get them to guess where the head is going to appear next. After he fools them a few times they move the box along the parade route to another location.

BOXING MATCH

Number of Clowns: Three

Characters: Two boxers (Mighty Max and Willie the Wienie), Referee

Costumes: Boxers wear shorts, tights, and tank tops. Referee wears black/white striped long sleeved shirt, black pants, and black bow tie. Boxers can also wear robes and towels over their trunks.

Props: Two stools, boxing gloves, bell, boxing ring

Stage: Empty boxing ring

The Performance ▬▬▬▬▬▬▬▬▬▬▬▬

Referee enters ring and announces: "Ladies and gentlemen, welcome to the fight of the century." He introduces Mighty Max: "From East Overshoe, Idaho, weighing 225 pounds, wearing blue trunks, the champion of the clown boxing world . . . Mighty Max!"

Mighty Max enters to music such as "Rocky." He is carrying his stool and steps into ring, shows his muscular body, and tries to get audience cheering for him. He greets Referee, and they establish fact that they are related.

Referee then introduces Willie the Wienie: "From Cupcake, New Hampshire, weighing 119 pounds soaking wet, wearing the mauve trunks, the challenger . . .Willie the Wienie!"

Willie enters, hesitatingly, carrying his stool, head down, shy, lacking self-confidence. He stumbles as he climbs over the ropes, barely making it. He lifts his arms slightly to get audience cheering for him. He is definitely the underdog.

Referee calls both boxers to the center of the ring for instructions: "On behalf of the boxing commission, and in memory of Otto Griebling, I want this to be a clean fight. I'll explain the rules. First, there will be no biting. (He demonstrates by biting Willie's arm. Willie screams and moves about as if in pain.) There will be no kicking. (He kicks Willie in the shins. Willie reacts.) There'll be no hitting below the belt. (He hits Willie) And finally, there'll be no eye-gouging. (He sticks fingers into Willie's eyes.) Now shake hands, return to your corners, and come out fighting when I ring the bell." Boxers reach forward to shake hands, but Mighty Max and the Referee shake hands, leaving Willie standing there. He shrugs his shoulders and returns to his corner, while Referee walks Mighty Max to his corner.

Mighty Max crosses the ring and sits down. Willie is slower getting to his corner. Just as Willie is about to sit down the Referee rings bell. Willie looks up, turns around and goes to the middle of the ring.

As both boxers meet in the center of ring Mighty Max swings at Willie and hits him good. (Use a fake hit. As Mighty Max swings, Willie candidly claps gloves together to make a noise, and then acts like he had just been hit.) Willie gets ready to hit back. Mighty Max reaches out and puts his hand on Willie's forehead. While Willie swings under Mighty Max's arm, not being able to reach him.

Mighty Max says, "Hold it a minute." They both stop.
Mighty Max takes another swing at Willie and again hits
him good. Mighty Max turns to return to his corner.
Willie chases, about to hit him, but the bell rings before
he can swing. Willie glares at the Referee as if to ask,
"What happened?"

Referee comes forward to send boxers to their respective
corners. Mighty Max sits down quickly while Referee
checks to see if he is okay, or if he needs anything.
Meanwhile, Willie goes slowly across the ring to his
stool. Just as he is about to sit down the Referee rings
the bell for the start of the second round.

Willie runs across ring with his glove raised, ready to
hit. Mighty Max sidesteps him and Willie runs past.
Willie turns around and again runs toward Mighty Max,
but Mighty Max puts up both hands to stop him. Mighty
Max points to the floor and asks, "What's that?" Willie
looks at the floor, and Mighty Max winds up and hits
him with uppercut. Willie spins around and falls. Mighty
Max heads back to his corner. Willie crawls across the
ring to try to catch up with him and hit him. Referee
comes up to Willie, puts his foot on him, forcing him to
the floor, and rings the bell over Willie's head.

Mighty Max sits in his corner, while Willie crawls
across floor to his stool. Just as he is about to sit down,
the bell rings to start round three.

The boxers glare at each other across the ring. They take
one step toward each other, then another, then another.
They are stalking each other. As they are about to touch,
they put their arms up and begin to dance together while

waltz music is played. After two turns around, they stop and separate.

Mighty Max hits Willie. Willie returns the punch. Hits are exchanged several times. Willie ducks and the Referee is knocked down. Willie then swings and knocks Mighty Max out. With both Mighty Max and the Referee on the floor, Willie stands with his foot on his opponent and declares himself the winner. Willie seeks crowd approval as the underdog and winner.

The End

Alternate Ending 1: The Referee and Mighty Max get up. They get into argument and Mighty Max pulls the long shirt off of the Referee. The Referee's pants drop and he chases Max off.

Alternate Ending 2: Mighty Max gets up and goes off with Willie (they are now friends, since the Referee is knocked out). Two additional clowns come on carrying a break-away stretcher. They roll the Referee onto stretcher, pick up stretcher poles, and leave with the Referee still lying there on the floor (on the stretcher cover). A moment passes before the Referee discovers he isn't being carried off. He sits up, yells, and chases stretcher bearers off.

Acknowledgement: My thanks to Jim Howle and Kenny Ahern for helping develop some of the elements of this skit.

BUSY BEE   (Three Persons)

Number of Clowns: Three

Characters: Clowns A, B, and C

Costumes: Regular clown wardrobe

Props: Chair, glass of water

Stage: Chair downstage in center, glass of water on floor behind chair

Setting: Clown A enters looking for partner. Calls for partner, looks to each side of stage, still calling for the other clown.

The Performance ▬▬▬▬▬▬▬▬▬▬

Clown A: *(Looks at audience.)* Have you seen _____? He was supposed to meet me here. *(Keeps looking around for partner.)* We were going to play a game. Maybe you've heard of it. It's called Busy Bee. I love that game. *(Still looking.)* But I don't see him here to play it on . . . I mean with.

Clown B: *(Enters looking around, not noticing Clown A on the stage.)*

Clown A: Ahem. Hey _____, wanna play a game?

Clown B: What kind of game?

Clown A: A really fun game.

Clown B: I guess I could play. What's it called? How do you play it?

Clown A: It's called Busy Bee. Now, see this chair?

Clown B: Yeah.

Clown A: Well it's not really a chair. It's a throne. And you get to sit on it because you're the Queen Bee.

Clown B: On, no you don't. I'm not going to be a QUEEN.

Clown A: But that just means you're the boss—the ruler. Don't you wanna be the boss?

Clown B: Well, all right—the ruler. Could I be a yard stick instead?

Clown A: No, you just be the ruler.

Clown B: Okay, but no funny stuff.

Clown A: Oh, no. Now you just sit here on your throne and get comfortable. Now, I'm the worker bee. I fly all over collecting honey. You do like honey, don't you?

Clown B: Oh yes, I love honey.

Clown A: Good. Then when I get back to you, I'll go umuh, umuh, umuh *(or your own sound effect)*, and you say, "Busy bee, busy bee, what have you got in the hive for me?" Then I give it to you. See? Isn't that a fun and easy game?

Clown B: I guess so.

Clown A: Now you stay right here, and I'll go and gather the honey. *(Clown B flies around gathering the* *honey, gets a mouthful of water, then returns.)*

Clown B: Busy bee, busy bee, what have you got in the hive for me?

Clown A: *(Spits water on Clown B.)*

Clown B: *(Gets up mad and embarrassed.)* I don't like this game. I'm not going to play it anymore.

Clown A: Wait. It's really a fun game. Let's see if you can play it on someone else.

Clown B: *(Thinks it over.)* Well, okay. I think I can do that.

Clown C: *(Enters looking around, not aware of other two clowns.)*

Note: While Clown B is interacting with Clown C, Clown A is on the sidelines encouraging Clown B to trick the new clown. Clown A can interject some lines if he wants to, but it is not necessary.

Clown B: Hey, friend. Do you like games?

Clown C: Well I like some games. What kind of game are you talking about?

Clown B: A really fun game. You'll like it. It's called Busy Bee and you're the boss. The Queen Bee. You don't have to do anything but sit here on the throne. I'll do all the work. *(Winks at audience.)*

Clown C: I just sit here and be the Queen Bee—the boss?

Clown B: Yep. And I'll do all the work. I fly around and gather all the honey from the flowers and then I come back and give it to you.

Clown C: Well how does it work?

Clown B: Well after I fly all around and gather the honey, I come back and stand right here *(at side of chair)* and go, "Umuh, umuh, umuh." Then you say, "Busy bee, busy bee, what have you got in the hive for me?" And I give it to you. You'll get all the honey.

Clown C: All of it?

Clown B: Every last drop of it.

Clown C: Well okay, I'll sit right here and be the Queen Bee. You fly around and get the honey.

Clown B: *(Flies around and gathers the honey and a mouthful of water from glass behind chair. He comes up to the side of chair.)* Umuh, umuh, umuh.

Clown C: *(Does not respond. Just looks around the room, oblivious to Clown B's presence.)*

Clown B: *(Louder and more emphatic.)* Umuh, umuh, umuh.

Clown C: *(Sits there looking around. Looks at Clown B but still does not respond.)*

Clown B: *(Swallows water.)* Hey, you're not playing fair. You're supposed to say, "Busy bee, busy bee, what have you got in the hive for me?"

Clown C: Oh, I'm sorry. I guess I forgot. I'll do it right this time.

Clown B: Well okay. I'll try again. *(Goes through flying bit again and gets more water. Comes back to side of chair.)* Umuh, umuh, umuh.

Clown C: *(Still ignores Clown B.)*

Clown B: *(Very angry, swallows water.)* I'm not playing anymore. You don't play fair.

Clown C: Oh, let's try one more time. I must have been thinking of something else.

Clown B: Well, only one more time. And you better get it right this time.

Clown C: I'll be very careful to do it right.

Clown B: *(As before, goes around flying gathering honey, and gets mouth of water, but while B is flying around, Clown C turns around and gets a mouthful of water from the glass. Clown B returns to side of chair.)* Umuh, umuh, umuh.

Clown C: *(Ignores him again.)*

Clown B: *(Very upset, swallows water.)* You're supposed to say, "Busy bee, busy bee, what have you got in the hive for me?"

Clown C: *(Gets up, stands on chair, and spits water at Clown B.)* I've played this game before and I knew what to do. Isn't it fun? *(Clowns A and C congratulate each other on getting Clown B again.)*

Clown B: *(Very embarrassed and mad, chases the other two clowns off the stage. Clown B carries the chair as a way to empty the stage for following acts.)*

The End

Acknowledgement: This skit has been performed by many clowns, but I attribute it's popularity to the following clowns: Leon "Buttons" McBryde, Earl "Mr. Clown" Chaney, Jim Howle, and Don "Homer" Burda. They have embellished the versions described in this book, and are a delight to watch.

DENTIST (Toothache)

Number of Clowns: Three (may also be performed by four)

Characters: Dentist (Dr. I. M. Painless), Dental Assistant, Patient, Friend (optional)

Costumes: Lab coat for the Dentist, nurse costume for Dental Assistant (clown in drag with balloons for bosom and butt)

Props: Large tools (pliers, hammer, screwdriver, needle, stethoscope), chair, foam tooth, bottle of water with "XXX" written on the front, spittoon (flashpot), tray for tools, bandanna, pieces of Styrofoam

Stage: Chair in the center of the stage, dentist's signs. Large spittoon-like pot is on the floor about 10 feet away from the chair.

Setting: Patient, accompanied by Friend, enters holding his jaw and wearing large bandanna around his head. (Large foam tooth is inside of bandanna.) Patient is moaning and groaning. After a few yells, he and his friend call for the doctor.

The Performance

Dentist: *(Enters and begins to examine the patient's friend. Friend objects to being examined and directs doctor to the actual patient.)* I can't do anything without my Dental Assistant.

Patient: *(Continues to moan in the background as the Dental Assistant enters and talks to Dentist.)*

Dental Assistant: Dr. Painless, I think he needs a shot before you begin.

130

Dentist: You're right. That's what we need, a shot. *(Takes out a bottle with x's on it and takes a drink.)*

Dental Assistant: No, Doctor not that kind of shot.

Dentist: *(Spits the liquid at the spittoon, which explodes since it is actually a flashpot.)* Whew! That's some kind of shot. Well, I guess we'd better get busy. I think you'd better administer some anesthetic to our friend here.

Dental Assistant: *(Takes out a large hammer and hits patient's friend over his head knocking him out.)*

Patient's Friend: *(He falls to floor and lays there.)*

Dentist: Not him. The patient, the patient.

Dental Assistant: *(Puts Patient into the chair and proceeds to knock him out in the same manner.)*

Dentist: Hand me the hammer and chisel. This looks like a major problem.

(Dental Assistant gives him the tools and Dentist proceeds to use them inside the patient's mouth. While working, with his back to the audience, the Dentist puts bits of Styrofoam into the patient's mouth. Each time after the Dentist chisels, the patient spits out bits of Styrofoam.)

Dentist: Let me have the pliers. I'll have to pull this tooth.

Dental Assistant: *(Gives him the large pliers.)* Say, Doctor. Do you know what time it is?

Dentist: *(Looks at watch.)* It's time to pull the tooth.

Patient's Friend: *(Recovering, gets up off the floor)*

Dentist, Dental Assistant, and Patient's Friend: *(They join hands, circle the patient and sing.)* "It's time to pull the tooth. . . . It's time to pull the tooth . . . It's time to pull the tooth."

Dentist: *(Looks at audience.)* I'm going to pull the tooth, the whole tooth, and nothing but the tooth.

(Dentist and Dental Assistant gather around the patient with their backs to the audience as they proceed to pull the tooth. They maneuver many ways in their effort. Dentist finally emerges with the foam tooth inside the jaws of the pliers, and turns to show it to the audience. Awakes and gets up, still holding jaw, moaning)

Dentist: *(To patient.)* What's the matter now?

Patient: You pulled the wrong tooth! *(Patient and friend chase the doctor and nurse off the stage.)*

The End

THE JUGGLERS

Number of Clowns: Three (can also be performed by two clowns)

Characters: Jugglers (Clowns A, B, and C)

Costumes: Regular clown wardrobe

Props: Juggling equipment, scarves, balls, clubs, large bowl, container of water, small table

Stage: Empty

Setting: Clown A enters, greets audience, and begins to juggle scarves.

The Performance

Clown B: Hey. I see you can juggle scarves.

Clown A: Yep, and I'm really good.

Clown B: That's no big deal. To be a juggler you have to juggle beanbags. *(Begins to juggle beanbags.)*

Clown A: Oh, yeah? Well, I think that to be a juggler, you have to juggle balls. *(Begins to juggle balls, while Clown B watches,)*

Clown C: *(Enters and watches Clown A.)* Do you guys really think you're jugglers?

Clown B: We sure do. We can juggle balls, beanbags, and scarves.

Clown C: Well, that's amateur stuff. Real jugglers juggle clubs. *(Juggles three clubs.)*

Clown B: Well that's no big deal. I can juggle four balls. *(Juggles four balls, or beanbags.)*

Clown A: I was just fooling you guys. I can really do some exotic juggling.

Clown C: Exotic juggling? What's that.

Clown A: I can do water juggling. Have you ever seen that?

Clown B: No, I've never seen it, and I don't think I ever will.

Clown A: Well, I can juggle water. I'll go get my stuff and show you. *(Exits to get small table, small bowl, and water container.)*

Clown B: *(To Clown C.)* Do you really think he can do it?

Clown C: Water juggling? What a joke. Nobody can juggle water.

Clown A: *(Returns, sets up table, pours water into bowl, flexes fingers, and prepares to juggle water.)* Ready, now? Indian water juggling. *(Builds up event.)*

Clowns B and C: *(Lean in to watch closely.)*

Clown A: *(Puts both hands into the water and begins splashing as if juggling, getting Clowns B and C very wet. They step back, call Clown A a fake, and chase him off.)*

The End

JUST ONE HAND

Number of Clowns: Three

Characters: Clowns A, B, and C

Costumes: Regular clown wardrobe

Props: One glass of water, one saucer, one small table

Stage: Table is set near center stage

Setting: Clowns A and B are on stage after a bit of clown business. Clown C enters carrying a glass of water on a saucer.

The Performance

Clown C: Hey fellows. I know you've been working very hard tonight, and the management wants to thank you. They sent you this ice cold glass of water.

Clown A: Oh, great. I'm really thirsty.

Clown B: Me too. I'll have that.

Clown A: Wait a minute. They sent that glass for me.

Clown B: I don't see your name on it.

Clown C: Hmmm, we seem to have a problem. One nice cold glass of water and two clowns. I'll have to think of some way to solve this problem. *(Thinks for a moment.)* I know. We'll have a contest to see which one of you can drink it with just one hand.

Clown A: I can do that. I always drink my water with just one hand.

Clown B: Me too. I never need two hands to drink a glass of water.

Clown C: Well, if you two are so sure of yourselves, here's the way the contest will work. I'll place the glass of water on this table, but before either of you can have it, you'll have to win the contest. You two stand back to back. I'll count to ten, and you each take ten steps. When you take the ten steps, remain facing away from the table. When I say go, then turn around and you race to this table to get the water. But remember, you can only use one hand.

Clown A: Sounds good to me. I can do that.

Clown B: I'm faster, so I'm sure I'll win.

Clown C: Okay. Get back to back and start to walk when I count. *(Begins to count to ten. While counting he takes the saucer from the bottom of the glass and places it on the top of the glass. He then turns the glass of water over so that it now is resting on the saucer, with the water inside. He places the saucer and glass on the table.)* Ready? Turn around and GO!

Clowns A and B: *(Turn and race to the table. They reach for the glass, but each stops when they see that the glass in inverted.)*

Clown A: *(To Clown B.)* You were really fast. I think you should have the glass of water.

Clown B: No, you said you were really thirsty. You can have it. *(They continue to try to give it to each other.)*

Clown C: *(Interrupts)* Hey, can I have the water if I can drink it with just one hand?

Clown A: Sure. If you can do it.

Clown B: But you can only use one hand.

Clown C: I can do that. *(He lifts the glass of water by holding the saucer by one edge, keeping the water upright. He leans his head back as far as he can, and places the bottom of the saucer on his forehead. He then lets go of the saucer and grasps the upside down glass by the side. Using pressure, he holds the glass against the saucer as he straightens his head, and turns the glass right side up. He places the glass on the table and removes the saucer, which is now on the top of the glass. He steps in front of the table and look to audience.)* See. I could do it with just one hand.

Clown A: *(Clown A steps forward, takes the glass and drinks the water.)*

Clown C: *(Turns around and sees Clown A drinking the water.)*

Clown A: I'm doing it with just one hand.

Clown C: *(Chases Clowns B and A from the stage.)*

The End

LEVITATION

Number of Clowns: Three (can also be performed by two clowns)

Characters: Hypnotist, Stooge, Clown

Costumes: Cape and turban for Hypnotist, regular clown wardrobe for others

Props: Bench seat, blanket or sheet, sticks with clown shoes fastened on the ends of them

Stage: Bench is set up in center, sheet covers shoes and bench

The Performance

Clowns enter stage, one wearing hypnotist outfit. With a lot of flourish, he indicates that he will hypnotize his assistant (the Stooge). If there is a third clown, two of them stand in line with hypnotist, the third clown behind the Stooge.

The Hypnotist throws his fingers toward the Stooge to hypnotize him. Nothing happens. The stooge looks like he can't be hypnotized. The Hypnotist tries again, without success. On the third try, the clown behind the Stooge falls down as if hypnotized.

The Hypnotist and the Stooge pick up the clown and place him, prone, on the bench. They carefully cover him with a sheet or blanket, at the same time placing fake feet (on sticks) out of the bottom of the sheet.

The Hypnotist stands back and attempts to levitate him. The hypnotized clown rises two or three inches and goes back down. Hypnotist tries again. Clown rises about six inches and goes back down.

The Hypnotist, getting anxious, puts all of the whammy he has into the spell and the Clown rises into a position where he appears to be standing. (Actually, he is holding the fake feet out of the bottom of the sheet. His own legs and feet are covered by the draping sheet.) He begins to float around as if he is levitated.

As he moves past the Stooge, the Stooge places his foot on the bottom of the sheet and it pulls off of the clown, revealing that he is actually holding the shoes on the sticks.

Exposed Clown and Hypnotist are chased from the ring.

The End

LITTLE SIR ECHO

Number of Clowns: Three

Characters: Clowns A, B, and C

Costumes: Regular clown wardrobe

Props: Curtain to hide Clown C, sign which reads: "Great Echo Cliff. Hear your voice 25 cents"

Stage: Empty

Setting: Clowns A and B enter the stage, as if touring the Grand Canyon and looking over the gorge. Clown A talks about Grand Canyon and how echoes return the words that are shouted out. Clown B wants to see how it works.

The Performance

Clown A: Wow! Just look at that. The Grand Canyon. *(Sees sign.)* And this must be the Great Echo Cliff. Let's put in a quarter and see how it works.

Clown B: Okay. It sure is big. I've never seen it before. How do echos work?

Clown A: You shout out something and it bounces off the other side of the canyon and comes back to you. Let me show you how it works. *(Deposits coin into box and shouts.)* Hello!

Clown C: *(Offstage acting as voice of an echo.)* Hello!

Clown B: Wow! That's really neat. Can I try some different words?

Clown A: Sure. Shout one out.

Clown B: *(Deposits coin then shouts.)* Cucumber!

Clown C: *(Echo)* Cucumber!

Clown A: See. It's really neat, isn't it? I'll do another one. *(Deposits coin and shouts.)* Chicken!

Clown C: (Echo) Chicken!

Clown B: Let me try another one. *(Deposits coin and shouts.)* Baloney! *(No return echo, just silence. Clowns wait for echo.)*

Clown A: Try it again.

Clown B: *(Deposits another coin.)* Baloney! *(No response.)*

Clown A: Why don't you try something different. Maybe a whole sentence.

Clown B: *(Thinks, deposits another coin, then shouts.)* I'm the funniest clown in the world!

Clown C: *(Echo)* Baloney! *(Peeks out from behind curtain, then goes over to take money from the box. Clown B see Clown C, knows it's a fraud and chases Clown C from the stage, with Clown A following the other two.)*

The End

NIAGARA FALLS

Number of Clowns: Three
Characters: Clown A (Trickster), Clown B, Clown C
Costumes: Regular Clown wardrobe
Props: Funnel, water pitcher, quarter, hot-water bottle
Stage: Empty
Setting: Clown A enters and speaks to audience.

The Performance

  Clown A: I learned a really neat trick and I'd like to show it to you, but I need a really dumb person to play it on. I know, let's play the trick on _____. Will you help me call for him?

(Audience response.)

Clown B: *(Answers in response to being called.)* Hi. We're you guys calling me?

Clown A: Yeah, _____. I learned a new game, and thought you might like to play it.

Clown B: Oh, great. I like new games. How do we play it?

Clown A: Well first, let me tell you about the prize. Have you ever heard of Niagara Falls?

Clown B: Sure. That's a really neat place. I want to go there sometime.

Clown A: This is your lucky day. If you win this game, I'll give you a free trip to Niagara Falls.

142

Clown B: Wow! Let's play. Tell me how to play.

Clown A: It's really pretty easy. All you have to do is place this funnel in your pants, tilt your head back, and put this quarter on your forehead. Then when I count to three you raise your head and drop the quarter into the funnel. That's all you have to do and you are the winner.

Clown B: I can do that. I just place the quarter on my forehead and drop it into this funnel?

Clown A: Yep. That's all you have to do. Here, put this funnel in you pants. *(Puts funnel into Clown B's pants.)* And here's the quarter.

Clown B: *(Tilts head back and places quarter on forehead.)*

Clown A: Now, I'll begin to count. Remember, you drop the quarter into the funnel when I count to three. Ready?

Clown B: Yep. I'm ready. Start counting.

Clown A: *(Takes a pitcher of water.)* Here we go—ONE, TWO . . . *(Pours water into the funnel, soaking Clown B's pants.)*

Clown B: Hey! You didn't tell me about that part of the game. I quit.

Clown A: Calm down, calm down. It's really a funny game. Wouldn't you like to play the trick, I mean the game, on someone else?

Clown B: Yes, but who would be that dumb?

Clown C: *(Enters stage.)*

Clown B: Hey _____ (Clown C). Do you wanna learn a new game?

Clown C: I guess so. How does it work?

Clown B: It's called Niagara Falls, and you can win a trip there if you win the game.

Clown C: Sounds good. I like to travel.

Clown B: Here's all you have to do. You put this funnel into your pants and then I pour water into it . . .

Clown A: *(Puts hand over Clown B's mouth to stop him and whispers into his ear.)*

Clown B: I mean you put this funnel into your pants and then you put this quarter on your forehead. I count to three and if you can drop the quarter into the funnel, then you win.

Clown C: I think I can do that. Let's try it. Do I really win the trip?

Clown B: Yep. Put the quarter on your head and we'll start.

Clown C: *(Puts the funnel into his pants and the quarter on his forehead.)*

Clown B: Here we go—ONE . . . *(Starts to pour water but gets no reaction.)* TWO . . . *(Pours more water into* *funnel without reaction.)* THREE . . . *(Clown C lifts his forehead and drops the quarter into the funnel.)*

Clown C: I did it. Now where's my prize?

Clown B: Wait. How come you didn't get wet?

Clown C: *(Takes hot water bottle out of pants, revealing that funnel was actually placed in top of hot water bottle.)* I've been to Niagara Falls before. Now where's my prize?

Clown B: I'll go get it. *(Runs off stage with Clowns A and C chasing him.)*

The End

WELCOME PARTY

Number of Clowns: Three

Characters: Clowns A, B, and C

Costumes: Normal clown wardrobe

Props: Two chairs, door

Stage: Chairs set up in living room

Setting: Clowns A and B are sitting together in the living room, front door is slightly ajar.

The Performance

Clown A: Hey, would you close the door? It's COLD outside.

Clown B: Sure. I'll close it. *(Goes to the door. He shuts the door, pauses briefly, opens the door back up, sticks his nose outside, and closes the door. He pause briefly, opens the door, sticks his nose outside, and closes it again.)*

Clown B: Hey, it didn't do any good.

Clown A: Why not?

Clown B: It's STILL cold outside.

Clown A: It's still cold outside? Of course it . . .

Clown C: *(Knocks on door.)*

Clown A: Who could that be?

(Clowns A and B go to the door.)

Clown C: Hi! I just moved in next door and we'd like to have a get-to-know-your-neighbors party.

Clown A: That would be nice.

Clown B: Yes, that sounds like fun.

Clown C: Nothing too fancy. Maybe a few steaks, some wine, music, a triple layer chocolate cake, and lots of ice cream.

Clown A: Great!

(Clowns A and B nod their heads in agreement.)

Clown C: Just myself and the wife and four or five of our friends.

Clown A: Sounds great.

Clown C: Next Saturday?

Clown A: Right

Clown C: What time shall we be here?

Clown A: Be HERE? . . . I thought it was YOUR party.

Clown C: Heck no. I can't afford all that stuff.

(Clowns A and B chase Clown C off stage.)

The End

FOUR
OR
MORE
CLOWNS

CLOWN AEROBICS

Number of Clowns: Seven (but could include more)

Characters: Aerobics Instructor and several students

Costumes: Workout (exercise) clothing

Props: Various workout equipment bags, water bottles, etc.

Stage: Empty

Music: Any upbeat exercise music. Preferably a popular tune known by your audience. Be sure music is long enough for entire act.

The Performance

During the class, the group should be arranged on the stage with everyone facing audience, perhaps in two lines, with instructor in front of group, also facing audience. Music begins with stage empty, and students wander in looking tired, bored, and not wanting to do aerobics. They greet each other gloomily, and with little enthusiasm. Some bring tote bags (carrying various props), and place them at the back of the stage.

Instructor enters energetically and greets students, "Hey, everyone, are we all set to exercise? Let's get those kinks out." Students moan and groan and make faces indicating that they really don't want to exercise.

Instructor says, "Oh my, it looks like many of you are still asleep. Are you sure you're ready for this?" Looks to audience "Do you think they're ready?" Encourages audience to respond. Instructor gets students into line to start warm-ups.

"Okay class, let's all line up and exercise. Ready? Let's begin. First neck rolls to the right." Instructor rolls head around in clockwise circle, counting for the class. "Now to the left." Instructor reverses direction of the head rolls and continues counting. While the Instructor is doing head rolls, the class is imitating, but staggering around as if dizzy.

> *Note:* It is very important that Instructor never looks back at the students during this skit. She should just assume that everyone is following her and not be aware of the goofiness that is occurring behind her.

"Now circles with the arms." Put arms out to sides, shoulder height, and begin to make large circles in a clockwise direction. Instructor counts. "Reverse the direction." The class, which is behind the Instructor, is doing different kind of circles. Class members are turning around in circles, not just rotating their arms. They have their hands up, with index fingers making little circles, while their whole bodies are turning circles. When Instructor says "reverse," they turn in opposite directions.

"Okay everyone, now we'll do toe touches." Instructor counts as she touches her toes, or tries to. Class, instead, touches each others toes, without bending down to touch them.

"Now, we'll move on to windmills." Instructor begins counting. (Windmills are done by extending the arms out to sides, and turning the entire upper portion of the body at waist, from one side to the other.) After several counts of windmills: "Let's really swing it out." Instructor adds a bit of bounce in the knees while doing windmills. While the Instructor is demonstrating this routine, the students are doing their own thing. They are really swinging, they are square dancing, skipping together and swinging around on each other's arms.

"We're ready for some stretching exercises. Everyone with arms over your heads." Instructor puts arms over her head, clasping hands, and bends to the right side as far as possible. She straightens up, and bends to the left side counting as she does the exercise.

"Really stretch it out." While the Instructor is stretching it out, students are stretching in another manner, by pulling each others arms, perhaps stretching the sleeves of shirts, or pants.

"Everybody run in place." Class actually does this, at least at the start. While they are jogging, one of the students stops, goes back to the her tote bag and gets some chips or popcorn to eat. This should be the one student most in need of the exercise. Still jogging, the entire class, except the one eating, huddles together. Entire huddle moves to opposite side of stage from the eater, then one of the noneaters taps the Instructor and points to the eater. This is the first time that the Instructor has looked back at the class.

Instructor jogs over to the snacker to take appropriate action. "What is going on? What are you doing?" Offender shrugs and indicates she was tired. Offers some snacks to Instructor. Instructor grabs the entire bag. "Give me those!" Instructor throws the bag on the floor, in disgust. Snacker had a big handful before the bag was taken away from her. When Instructor turns around, snacker puts more food into her mouth. Instructor grabs last bit of food and throws it to the floor.

"Now, everyone get back in line and let's continue with the exercise." Instructor returns to her place in front of the students, and gives the class time to get back into lines and into the exercise. "Now it's time to begin the cool down exercises. Breath in deep." Instructor raises arms over her head as she breaths in. "And, exhale and down." Brings arms back down to sides. Class imitates this portion exactly with instructor.

Raises arms again. "And one toe touch before we quit." Instructor bends forward to touch toes, but can't get back up. Has thrown back out and can't straighten out. Meanwhile, class is beginning to leave. They gather up their belongings and some leave.

"Wait. Don't leave. I can't straighten up. I've thrown my back out." Students continue to socialize with each other, and don't even hear the instructor. Finally a couple of large, strong, members see the Instructor and come to her aid. They look at the situation, and devise a plan. They pick the Instructor up, being sure she holds her position and does not straighten up. They turn her, so that her shoes are now facing the audience. On the bottom of the shoes are the words THE END. They carry her off the stage as the music ends.

The End

Acknowledgement: This skit was first performed at the 1986 Texas Clown Association convention. It was written by Mauri Norris, Charles McBride, Mary Lostak, Bill McDaniel, Bill Strickland, Kathy Davis, and Kathy Pierce.

CONSTRUCTION COMPANY

Number of Clowns: Six

Characters: Mother, Brat, Construction Foreman, three workers

Costumes: Construction outfits, hard-hats, small child and mother outfits

Props: Two sawhorses, break-away ladder, board (for swings), plank, chair, tarp, wheelbarrow, hard-hats, blueprints, foam blocks, stepladder, single ladder

Stage: Empty

The Performance

Mother is sitting in a chair knitting, while her child (Brat) is playing on floor with foam blocks. Foreman enters with blueprints. Mother and Foreman look at them. Brat comes over and steals prints away. Other workers are spreading tarp on floor. Mother goes to child to scold him and get prints back.

After workers spread tarp, one goes to chair and moves it about 10 feet. Mother attempts to sit back down, on missing chair, and lands on the floor. She gets up and looks around for the chair. Finds it and sits down. Brat pulls tarp, causing everyone standing on it to fall.

Worker brings in stepladder and sets it in center of the stage. Brat throws block at worker, hitting him on the back. Block bounces off. Worker falls. Mother gets up and scolds Brat. Another worker moves her chair. She again plans to sit, but falls onto the floor. She gets up, finds chair, and sits down. Other workers enter with two sawhorses and place a plank across the top, with one end hanging over. A worker is standing near the end. Brat comes over and pushes him. He pushes back. Brat pushes worker backward and he sits on the plank, causing it to flip up and hit foreman (who is just coming over).

Both Foreman and worker are on the ground. Another worker enters carrying board under his arm. He turns around (board swings), and just about hits the other two, but they duck in time. They sit up, board swings back and knocks them down. They get up and take board out.

Worker begins to work with stepladder. He climbs it. Sits on top, straddling the top. Brat comes over and starts to push ladder over. At first he pushes it, then pulls it back, then finally pushes it over. Worker on top rides ladder to the floor, and does forward roll.

Another worker enters with a break-away ladder and goes for Brat's neck. While ladder rails go past kid's neck, the rungs of the ladder fall onto the floor. (The break-away ladder is made with only the top three rungs glued in. Other rungs are held in place with Velcro on their ends so they fall off when they touch the Brat's neck.)

Two workers come in with another single ladder, which they carry between them, above their heads. They encourage the Brat to hang on to the rungs, then they lift the ladder high. Worker places wheelbarrow under Brat. They tickle Brat so he falls into the wheelbarrow, which could be filled with foam or soap. They wheel the Brat off, with the others chasing.

The End

CURING MACHINE

Number of Clowns: Seven

Characters: Doctor, Nurse (Miss. Sippi), Patients (1, 2, 3, and 4), nurse's boyfriend (Ray)

Costumes: Doctor's coat, nurse's uniform, regular clown wardrobe

Props: Curing machine (has a lot of flashing lights and dials), one chair

Stage: Doctor's office, with interesting machine in the middle of the room, and one chair.

Setting: Doctor comes out of his office into waiting room.

The Performance

Doctor: Miss. Sippi, will you come in here for a minute?

Nurse: Yes, Doctor.

Doctor: I want to show you our new machine that cures any illness.

Nurse: *(Doctor and Nurse look at machine.)* That's wonderful doctor. How does it work?

Doctor: Why, you take this cap and put it on a patient, like this. *(Puts cap on Nurse.)* Then you transfer the illness of the patient into the dummy.

Nurse: And where's the dummy?

Doctor: It hasn't come in yet. We have the shipping papers, but it hasn't arrived.

156

Nurse: Well, that certainly looks like a wonderful invention—if it works. (Nurse's boyfriend enters.)

Nurse: Hello, Raymond.

Ray: Hi Sally. Hi Doc. Just dropped by for a minute on my way back to the store.

Nurse: While you're here, let me show you this new machine we've just received. The Doctor tells me it will cure anything. Here's how it works. You put the cap on this way *(puts cap on him)*, and the illness of the patient is transferred to the dummy.

Ray: Where's the dummy?

Nurse: It hasn't arrived yet.

Doctor: *(Listening to outer office.)* Say, Miss Sippi. I believe there's a patient arriving. Please check the waiting room to see. *(To Raymond.)* Quick, Raymond, let me hook you over here where the dummy is supposed to be, so I can try the machine on this patient.

Ray: Oh, no you don't. I'm feeling really good and I want to stay that way.

Doctor: I'll pay you ten dollars per patient if you sit over there and pretend you're the dummy.

Ray: That's more like it. I'll give it a try.

Doctor: Hurry now. *(Attaches machine to Raymond.)*

Patient 1: *(Entering, with his hand up in the air.)*

Doctor, my hand is giving me some trouble. I've heard that you have a new machine that can help me. Will you try it?

Doctor: Sure. Just let me put this cap on your head, and we'll try the machine. *(Puts cap on patient, turns machine on. Suddenly Raymond raises his hand and Patient brings his hand down.)* It worked. See, you're cured.

Patient 1: Thanks Doc. You're new machine is great. Here's twenty-five dollars.

Doctor: Thank you. Be sure to tell other people about our new machine.

Nurse: You have another patient, doctor. Shall I send her in?

Doctor: Sure, nurse. We're all ready.

Patient 2: *(Jerking)* Doctor, Doctor I have a nervous affliction. I can't stop jerking. If you can help me, I'll give you one hundred dollars.

Doctor: Well, thank you my friend. I have this brand new machine, which I'm sure will cure you of your affliction. Let me put this cap on your head and we'll give it a try. *(Doctor puts cap on the Patient, turns on the machine. The Patient stops jerking, but Raymond starts jerking, with his hand still up in the air.)* See, you're cured.

Patient 2: Thanks, Doctor. Here's the money I promised. *(Pays and leaves.)*

158

Nurse: Doctor, your fame is spreading. I have another patient.

Doctor: Send him in. This machine is wonderful.

Patient 3: *(Enters)* Doctor. I've had a awful time. I was kicked by a mule, and ever since then I've been pawing the ground. See. *(Paws ground.)* If you can cure me, I'll give you two hundred dollars.

Doctor: Let's see if my new machine can help you. Take a seat and let me put this cap on your head. *(Puts cap on Patient. Turns on machine. Patient stops pawing ground and Raymond begins, adding this problem to the other ones he has acquired.)* See, you're cured already.

Patient 3: Thank you, doctor. You've helped me a lot. *(Pays and leaves.)*

Nurse: There's another patient to see you doctor. A young woman.

Doctor: Send her in, nurse.

Patient 4: *(Enters. She is very pregnant.)* Doctor, I've been having a problem pregnancy and I wonder if you can help me.

Raymond: *(Sees her, takes off the connections.)* Oh no! I've don't mind these too much, but I'm not going to become pregnant. I'm oughtta here. *(Runs off stage.)*

Doctor: *(Turns off machine, and he and Patient Four chases Raymond off the stage.)*

The End

DENTIST'S WAITING ROOM

Number of Clowns: Ten

Characters: Dental Assistant, Dentist, screaming Kid, Kid's Mom, Big Guy (sissy), Patients (1, 2, 3, 4, and 5)

Costumes: Nurse's uniform for Dental Assistant, dentist's jacket for Dentist, regular clown wardrobe for others

Props: Chairs, old magazines, "Waiting Room" sign, "Dentist" sign, large tooth with legs, flat bi-fold with window and door, large foam sucker with Velcro on one side

Stage: Bi-fold screen is set up with door, five chairs are setup for patients.

Setting: Patients 1, 2, and 3 are sitting in the waiting room reading magazines. A mother enters with little screaming Kid. The Kid begins annoying the other patients (kicking them, taking magazines, etc.) Each patient is called into the dentist's office during the skit. When they come out, they are seemingly relieved of their pain.

The Performance

Dental Assistant: *(Enters from the examination room.)* Mrs. Jones, the dentist will see you now.

Patient 1: *(Stands up and walks into the examination room.)*

Kid: *(Goes over to Patient 2 and takes a magazine from him.)* I want to look at that magazine. Mom, look at the nice picture on the cover.

160

Mom: Junior, give that magazine back to the man. He was reading it.

Kid: Waaah! I want the magazine.

Mom: *(Takes magazine and gives it back to the Patient.)*

Kid: *(Cries, then looks around for someone else to bother. Goes over and kicks Patient 3.)*

Patient 3: OW! Hey lady, can't you control that kid? *(Raises hand as if to clobber the kid, then holds leg where he was kicked.)*

Patient 1: *(Exits examination room.)* Oh, I feel so much better now. He's a wonderful dentist. *(Exits stage.)*

Dental Assistant: *(Calls Patient 2.)*

Patient 2: *(Goes into examination room.)*

Patient 4: *(Enters waiting room and takes a seat. Makes eyes at Kid and pretends to play hide-and-seek behind magazine with him.)* Hey kid. Come over here. I've got a sucker for you.

Kid: *(Goes over to Patient 4. Gets a large, bright-colored sucker and goes back to Mom, licking it.)*

Patient 2: *(Exits examination room, greatly relieved, and bids farewell to those in waiting room.)*

Big Guy: *(Enters waiting room and takes a seat far away from examination room door. He is afraid, and does not want to be here. He has a bandanna tied*

161

around his jaw, indicating a badly infected tooth.)

Dental Assistant: *(Calls Patient 3 to come into the examination room.)*

Patient 3: *(Enter examination room.)*

Kid: *(With Mom reading books and licking sucker.)*

Patient 5: *(Enters waiting room and sits down with others. Picks up a magazine and begins reading. Kid goes over and ties his shoes together.)*

Patient 3: *(Exits office very satisfied.)*

Dental Assistant: *(Calls Patient 4 into examination room.)*

Patient 4: *(When he passes the Kid, Kid smacks him in the butt with the sucker. Sucker sticks to Patient's pants, this is accomplished with a piece of Velcro on one side of the sucker. Patient enters examination room without knowing that sucker it stuck to him.)*

Kid: *(Happy about having pulled this trick on Patient 4.)*

Big Guy: *(Obviously very nervous about being here.)*

Patient 4: *(Exits examination room still wearing the sucker on his rear.)* I made a mistake, my appointment is for next week.

Dental Assistant: *(Calls Big Guy. He doesn't want to go. Dental Assistant tries to persuade him. Doesn't work. Solicits help from Patient 5. Together, they get Big Guy* *on his feet, and push him into the examination room.)*

Big Guy: *(Screams and cries from examination room. Finally exits wearing sticker. He smiles with one tooth missing.)* I was very good, the Dentist gave me a sticker.

Dental Assistant: *(Calls Patient 5 into examination room.)*

Patient 5: *(Trips when he gets up, because his shoes were tied together. He fixes them and enters examination room.)*

Kid: *(Laughs when Patient 5 trips. Only Mom and Brat are left in the waiting room. Mom tries to entertain the Kid as they wait.)*

Patient 5: *(Exits examination room and leaves.)*

Dentist: *(Exits examination room. Greets woman and bratty kid, establishing the fact that they are his wife and child. Kid is smiling and being very good. Dentist suggests they all go to the zoo, and thanks them for waiting while he was seeing patients.)*

The End

Alternate Ending: Big Guy exits examination room chased by a giant tooth with legs. Big Guy and tooth run from the waiting room, followed by all of the other patients in the waiting room.

As written, this skit is very basic. It is open to many interpretations and variations. Make changes to suit your group's size and abilities.

DIVIDING THE CHECK

Number of Clowns: Four

Characters: Waitress, three diners (Clowns A, B, and C)

Costumes: Waitress outfit, and normal clown wardrobe

Props: Table and three chairs, tablecloth and various items of food, tablet and pencil, play money, calculator

Stage: Table and three chairs

Setting: Three diners are finishing up their meal as the Waitress brings the check. She stands by them as they discuss the bill.

The Performance

Clown A: Ah, that was a good meal. I'm really full. *(Sees waitress approach.)* Oh, here's the check. *(Looks at it.)* Let's see. I had the chicken and coffee, so my amount comes to about $7.50.

Clown B: Let me see that. *(Takes the check.)* I had the ham and mashed potatoes so I guess I owe about $9.45. *(Hands check to Clown C.)*

Clown C: I had the hamburger and french fries and a large Coke. Hmmmm . . . How can my amount possible be $15.30? *(To waitress.)* I don't think this is right.

Clown A: It's right. Just pay the bill and let's get out of here.

Clown C: I still don't think it's right. *(Waitress looks at bill.)*

Waitress: It seems right to me. You had the super

164

duper large hamburger and the extra large portion of fries.

Clown A: Yeah, dummy. You had the big belly, so stop your belly-aching.

Clown C: I don't think it's right. *(Tosses glass of water at Clown A.)* And now you're all wet.

Clown A: Well, I'm all wet and not very happy about it. Let's see how you like it. *(Tosses glass of water on Clown C.)*

Clown B: *(Laughs)*

Clown C: *(Picks up ketchup and hit's the bottom of the bottle, squirting ketchup on Clown A.)*

Clown A: *(Picks up a plate and fork. Uses fork to shoot remaining food from plate onto Clown C.)*

Clown C: Well, I've had enough of your stuff. Put up your dukes.

Waitress: *(Walks by with tray full of cream pies.)*

Clown A: *(Takes a pie from the tray and plants it on Clown C's face.)*

Clown C: That's it! *(Takes pie and hits Clown A with it.)*

Clown B: *(Still laughing.)*

Clown C: *(Hits Clown B with pie.)*

Waitress: *(Goes out and comes back with more pies.)*

(Major pie fight ensues, with everyone, including Waitress, getting pied. Finally, clowns run out of restaurant.)

Waitress: Hey, wait! You forgot my tip. *(Leaves the stage, upset.)*

The End

DOCTOR BLUEBONNET

Number of Clowns: Six

Characters: Receptionist, Doctor, Patients 1, 2, 3, and 4

Costumes: Nurse and doctor outfits, regular clown wardrobe

Props: Desk and chair for Receptionist, four chairs for patients, wet sponge, note pad

Stage: Desk and chair on one side, patient chairs in center

Setting: Receptionist is sitting at desk, filing nails while waiting for patients to arrive. Patient 1 arrives, limping to Receptionist's desk.

The Performance ▬▬▬▬▬▬▬▬▬▬▬

Receptionist: What's wrong with you?

Patient 1: I stubbed my toe in a toe-may-toe patch.

Receptionist: Oh, just sit down. Dr. Bluebonnet is coming in soon. He'll look at it.

(Patient 1 sits down, Patient 2 enters, whining.)

Patient 2: Oh . . . oh . . . the pain. I gotta see the Doc.

Receptionist: What's wrong?

Patient 2: I wrenched my ankle and it hurts like mad. *(Has wrench in sock, sticking out)*

Receptionist: Well, have a seat. Dr. Bluebonnet is coming in soon.

(Patient 2 takes a seat. Patient 3 enters with plastic faucet fastened to knee. Patient 3 is carrying wet sponge in a plastic bag, which is hidden from the audience.)

Patient 3: Oh . . . ow . . . oh . . . ow . . . I gotta see the doctor.

Receptionist: Now, what's wrong with you?

Patient 3: I got water on the knee.

Receptionist: Well, sit down. Dr. Bluebonnet will see you when he gets here.

Patient 4: *(Enters wearing a huge thumb.)* Ow . . . ow . . . oweee . . . I want the see the doctor right away.

Receptionist: Quit your bellyachin' and just sit down. Dr. Bluebonnet's coming in soon.

Doctor: *(Enters carrying notepad, crosses over in front of the patients, and goes to Receptionist's desk.)*

Receptionist: Hi, Dr. Bluebonnet. How are you today?

Doctor: I'm fine. Are these my patients? *(Gestures to patients sitting in chairs.)*

Receptionist: Yeah, they're your patients, because I don't have any.

Doctor: *(To first patient)* Good afternoon. And what's your problem?

Patient 1: Doctor, I stubbed my toe in a toe-may-toe patch.

Doctor: *(Thinks for a moment then writes on the note pad.)* I'm writing you a prescription to AAA.

Patient 1: For what?

Doctor: A tow truck. *(Doctor goes behind patient chairs, and talks to Patient 2.)* And what's your problem?

Patient 2: *(Points to ankle.)* It's my ankle. I wrenched it.

Doctor: Well, that sure puts a monkey wrench in the situation. Let's see if I can help. *(Takes the wrench and tightens patient's ankle.)*

Patient 2: Oh . . . oh . . . oh . . . whew. Now that feels better.

Doctor: *(To Patient 3.) And* you? What's your problem?

Patient 3: Oh, I have water on the knee.

Doctor: Did you try draining it?

Patient 3: No.

Doctor: I think I can fix that. *(Opens valve.)*

(Patient 3 discretely gives wet sponge to Doctor. Doctor squeezes sponge while opening valve to allow water to drip)

Doctor: *(Moves to end of row of chairs and talks to Patient 4)* And you, what's your problem?

Patient 4: *(Holds up big thumb.)* My thumb, my thumb, somebody stepped on it.

Doctor: Somebody stepped on it? Let me take a look. Let's see. *(Examines thumb.)* That's really thumbthing. I know what will take your mind off of it. *(Doctor stomps on patient's foot.)*

Patient 4: Ooooow!

Doctor: *(Looks up and sighs.)* Oh, this job is so hard. I think I need a rest. *(Doctor goes in front of patients and lays across all four laps and pretends to go to sleep.)*

Receptionist: *(Walks over to chairs and stands next to patients, holding the doctor)* So how do you all feel, now that you've seen Doctor Bluebonnet?

Patients 1, 2, 3, and 4: *(In unison.)* "Everything's better, with Blue Bonnet on it" *(They stand and Doctor falls to the floor. Patients run out and doctor gets up and chases them.)*

Acknowledgement: To Ron and Sue Kardynski for allowing me to see the humor in this one. I thought it was really stupid when I first saw it.

The End

FASHION SHOW

Number of Clowns: Six

Characters: Narrator, Clown Models A, B, C, D and E

Costumes: Spring suit (suit with various springs and slinky's on it), tank top (shirt with small tanks on it), cotton shorts and socks (cotton balls fastened on these), racquetball shoes (racquets fastened on tennis shoes), straw hat (drinking straws on hat), ball gown (various balls fastened on large dress), diamond necklace (card diamonds around the neck), diamond earrings (small diamond cards hanging on ears), five carrot ring (ring with five carrots on it), pin striped suit (suit with many large safety pins on it), top hat (hat with many toy tops on it), hose (garden hose in many colors), ladies pumps (couple of balloon pumps), tee-shirt (many tea bags fastened on it, plus various pieces of fruit), boxer shorts (large shorts with boxing gloves on them, cotton balls in inner lining)

Props: Lectern for Narrator, various costumes, potato sack with "SACCS" written on it

Stage: Lectern on one side for narrator

The Curtain Rises

Narrator enters, and goes to the podium. "Welcome, and thank you for attending our fashion show. Tonight I'm sure you'll be pleased and enthusiastic over our new line of clothing fashions designed by Kalvin Clown. Sit back and enjoy our review of these garments. Later we'll tell you where you can purchase these one-of-a-kind outfits. Let's begin with our latest spring combination."

171

Clown A enters, modeling spring outfit. "As you can see, _____ is wearing the perfect *spring* ensemble, just as the name implies. This outfit is available in short, medium, and long lengths, as well as numerous colors. _____ has chosen our basic gray. This outfit is available for men and women, and oh, how slinky it will make you look and feel. Moving from spring, it's time to think summer."

Clown B enters wearing tank top, cotton shorts and socks, racquetball shoes and straw hat. "_____ is seen in one of our new tank tops. What a cool, refreshing top to wear while leisurely working around the clowndominium, or perhaps enjoying your favorite sport—fishing or boating. She is also wearing a pair of 100 percent cotton shorts and cotton socks. She complements this outfit with racquetball shoes, and one of our new looks in straw hats. Truly an outdoor outfit. Thank you _____. With summer comes proms, gala events, and evenings on the town."

Clown C enters wearing ball gown. "What woman would not want to be seen in one of our gorgeous ball gowns? As you can see, this versatile gown can be worn on many distinguished occasions. We're sure everyone will be talking about you as you bounce from one person to another. You're bound to be the belle of the ball." (Narrator takes out small bell and rings it.) "_____ is also wearing one of our designer diamond necklaces with matching earrings, and an absolutely stunning five carrot ring. _____, take another spin around the stage. Now let's take a look at our more serious styles of clothing. For the man on the way up the ladder."

Clown D enters wearing pin striped suit. "_____
is modeling our version of the woman's pin-striped suit.
She has also chosen to top off her outfit with one of our
very distinguishable top hats. This outfit makes her truly
look like a top executive. She has also chosen one of
our newest shades of hose, to accent the outfit. We can
match any article of clothing with the many colors of
hose we have. To make the outfit complete, _____
also models a pair of our new ladies pumps. Truly a
very coordinated look. Thank you _____.

And last, but certainly not least, _____ is
modeling some of our latest undergarments." Clown E
enters wearing a Fruit-of-the-Loom tee-shirt. "As we say,
don't be a fruit, be a knockout, in our uniquely styled,
yet versatile underwear. The tee-shirt being modeled can
be worn around the house, on the golf course, or under
other shirts. Along with the Fruit-of-the-Loom tee-shirt,
is our version of boxer shorts. Our boxers don't feel
starchy, like cardboard, because they are cotton lined.
They are the greatest, just like all of our lines of clothing.

"Well, that concludes our fashion show tonight. I'm sure
you are all wondering where you can purchase these
remarkable outfits. Right now they are only available at
our store, the store on the avenue—Fifth Avenue. That's
right, SACCS." He holds up a potato sack. "Saccs, with
a double C, for Custom Clown Clothing. Before we
leave, lets bring our models back to allow you one more
look at our wonderful line of Kalvin Clown clothing."
All clown models return, do a turn on stage and leave.
Narrator concludes and leaves stage.

The End

Acknowledgement: This skit was originally written and performed by the Michigan Bell Clowns Galore, many years ago.

MR. KNOW-IT-ALL

Number of Clowns: Five

Characters: Mr. Know-it-All, Clowns A, B, C, and D

Costumes: A swami-turban for Mr. Know-it-All, regular clown wardrobe for others

Props: Two telephones, telephone stand, chair

Stage: Chair on one side with telephone on stand, one cellular telephone

Setting: Mr. Know-it-All enters and takes a seat on the chair. Begins to read a book. Clowns B, C, and D enter. Clown C has a newspaper.

The Performance

Clown C: Hey guys. Did you see this ad? Mr. Know-It-All is appearing at the local mall. He's supposed to be a very famous fortune teller and he's taking telephone calls from people. Let's call him and see how much he really does know. I have my cellular phone right here. We can call from here. *(Takes cellular phone from pocket or briefcase.)*

Clown B: Okay. I have a really good question for him. Let me see your phone. *(Picks up phone and dials.)* Let's see, the number is 1-900-NO-IT-ALL.

(Phone rings across. Mr. Know-it-All picks it up.)

Mr. Know-it-All: Mr. Know-it-All. I know everything about everything. What is your question?

Clown B: What's going to happen to me today?

Mr. Know-it-All: Well, you're clumsy and you'll have a big fall.

Clown B: *(Hands phone to Clown C.)* He's crazy. He doesn't know anything. *(Walks across stage, trips, and has a big fall.)*

Clowns B, C, and D: WOW! That's just what he said would happen. Maybe he's really a fortune teller.

Clown C: Let me talk to him. Hey, Mr. Know-it-all. You were pretty lucky with that one. What's going to happen to me?

Mr. Know-it-All: *(Thinks)* This is a hard one. I think you might lose some of your clothes.

Clown C: Lose some of my clothes? That doesn't make any sense. I don't know how that could happen.

(While Clown C is talking, Clown E is standing alongside of him. Clown E yawns and stretches his arms. When he swings arms back down, he accidently knocks the hat off of Clown C.)

Clowns B, C, and D: He was right again. He's really something.

Clown E: *(Takes the phone from Clown C.)* Let me talk to Mr. Know-it-All. Okay, wise guy. What's going to happen to me. *(Holds up a lottery ticket.)*

Mr. Know-it-All: Hmmmm . . . . I see you winning a large amount of money.

Clown A: *(Enters with newspaper.)* Hey, did you guys

see the lottery numbers in today's paper?

Clown D: No. What are they?

Clown A: Well, the numbers are 12, 29, 20, and 57.

Clown D: Those are my numbers. I win! I'm rich. Mr. Know-it-All really does know his stuff.

Clown A: Who are you talking to on the phone?

Clown B: That's Mr. Know-it-All. He can predict the future. Why don't you talk to him?

Clown A: Okay. I will. I'll really test this guy. Hey, Know-it-All.

Mr. Know-it-All: That's MISTER Know-it-All. What can I do for you?

Clown A: If you're so good, tell me what's going to happen to me.

Mr. Know-it-All: I see you sitting in a chair. You are leaning back and the chair falls over. You crash to the floor.

Clown A: That's crazy. You don't know anything. I'm not even sitting on a chair. Hey guys. This call is costing us a lot of money. (*Pushes button on telephone.*) Operator . . . operator . . . . please reverse the charges. (*Speaks to group of clowns.*) There, that will be cheaper. I reversed the charges.

(*Across the stage, Mr. Know-it-All leans back and falls off of chair on to the floor.*)

Clowns A, B, C, and D: *(Leave stage chatting and wondering about Mr. Know-it-All.)*

The End

Acknowledgement: This skit was written in a skit development class at the Madison, Wisconsin Clown Encounter, sponsored by Happy's Clown Alley, in November 1993. I don't remember all of the clowns, but Laffy and Taffy were instrumental in putting it together.

PHOTOGRAPHER

Number of Clowns: Four to eight

Characters: Photographer, Father, Mother, and one or more children

Costumes: Regular clown wardrobe

Props: Old fashioned camera (equipped to squirt powder and water, bird on stick, flash-pot on camera

Stage: Camera and chairs

The Performance

Photographer busies himself setting up the equipment and chairs for a family portrait. He uses an old fashioned camera with a cloth attached to the back of it. Camera also has a birdie and a flash pot.

Photographer sets up chairs for the family to sit on. There are several small chairs, and one large chair in the back.

The family arrives in a turmoil, and is cordially greeted by the photographer. The children sit in the little chairs, which are too small for them, while Mother sits in the large chair, with Father standing beside her, hat in hand.

Photographer finishes setting up the equipment while the children create all kinds of havoc. They fidget, make faces, get spanked, constantly blow their noses, chase each other around the chairs, pull at the girl's braids, fight, and generally make a nuisance of themselves.

Finally, all is quiet and the Photographer is ready to take the picture. He squirts powder out the front of the camera and everyone flinches and moves about. Photographer gets them back into order.

He returns to the camera, this time squirting water onto the family. They again fall back and are restored to order by the Photographer.

He waves the birdie and everyone smiles, outrageously, but at the last minute the Photographer decides to get more powder for the flash. When he leaves the camera, Mother gets up to see what the family looks like through the lens. She lifts the camera cloth, bends over and looks through the lens.

The photographer returns. He does not notice that Mother is missing, and tells the family to hold the position. He then picks up the cloth, which is actually Mother's black skirt. She panics, steps out and hits him with her purse. Father gets up, comes over, takes Mother by the hand, and leads her back to her chair.

Photographer gets under the cloth again and shouts "hold it" as the family freezes for the portrait. Photographer presses button, and there is a big explosion. When the smoke clears, the family is standing in tattered underwear. They shout and everyone chases the Photographer out of the ring.

The End

REDUCING MACHINE

Number of Clowns: Five

Characters: Machine Operator, Small Clown, Large Clown, Clown A, Clown B,

Costumes: Normal clown wardrobe, Large Clown and Small Clown dressed alike

Props: Large box (equipped with flash pot for explosives) painted with the words "REDUCING MACHINE," large hot dog, small hot dog, large cowboy hat, small cowboy hat,

Stage: Empty

Setting: Machine Operator pushes machine onto stage and speaks to audience. Small Clown is inside of the machine.

The Performance

Machine Operator: Ladies and gentlemen, let me introduce you to one of the latest marvels of mankind. This machine will eliminate storage problems. It can make large things small to make them easier to store. It will help you in many ways.

Clown A: *(Enters stage wearing large cowboy hat.)*

Machine Operator: Let me demonstrate. *(To Clown A)* Sir, would you come over here for a moment?

Clown A: *(Walks over to Machine Operator.)*

Machine Operator: *(Removes Clown's hat and places in into the reducing machine.)*

Large Clown: *(Wanders onto the stage and is interested in the machine. Gets in the way. Machine Operator pushes him aside and goes on with the demonstration.)*

Machine Operator: Let me demonstrate this wonderful machine. It will make your head a lot lighter after we fix that hat.

Clown A: *(Shows mild protest, but watches with interest as the hat is placed into the machine.)*

Machine Operator: *(Turns crank on the side of the machine. Looks into machine and removes small cowboy hat, which he gives back to Clown A.)*

Clown A: *(Puts on hat and walks away, somewhat satisfied.)*

Large Clown: *(Continues to show interest in machine and walks around inspecting it.)*

Clown B: *(Enters eating a very large hot dog.)*

Machine Operator: *(Walks over to Clown B, takes the hot dog, and puts into the machine.)*

Clown B: *(Wondering what is going to happen, goes to machine to watch.)*

(Large Clown is still in the way as he looks at the machine. He is pushed away by Machine Operator.)

Machine Operator: *(Places large hot dog into the top of machine, turns crank, removes small hot dog, and gives it to Clown B.)*

Clown B: *(Not to sure of what happened, continues to eat small hot dog, and walks away.)*

Large Clown: *(Now getting braver, opens the door of the machine and looks inside.)*

Machine Operator: *(Comes up behind Large Clown, pushes him into the machine, and closes the door. Turns crank, looks inside. Not satisfied, he turns crank more. Lifts top door and looks inside. Still not happy, turns crank more and sets off explosion.)*

(Door at opposite end of machine opens and Small Clown, dressed exactly like Large Clown, exits door. All run around ring and chase Small Clown from the ring. Machine is removed by stage hands with Large Clown still inside)

The End

SEASCAPE

Number of Clowns: Several (up to 12)

Characters: Storyteller, Sun, Cloud, Fisherman, Bathing Beauty, Waves, Lighthouse, Fish, Boater, Seagull, Breeze, Tide

Costumes: Fisherman, white cap, bathing beauty

Props: Large Tide Box, fishing pole, pictures of the sun, clouds, and a lighthouse

Stage: Empty

The Performance

Storyteller is the only one with a speaking part. He enters stage and informs audience that he is going to paint a beautiful picture for them. He begins by gesturing to them that his picture will be a beautiful landscape. He points out the lake, the wonderful sand beach, and the clear blue sky. He then says that only a few nice, fluffy clouds move across the sky.

A clown (Cloud-clown) enters the stage holding a large "cloud" in front of his face. Another clown (Sun-clown) enters stage *behind*, and hidden by, Cloud-clown. These two clowns take positions upstage center (the back).

Storyteller says, "The sun begins to peek out from behind the clouds." The Sun-clown looks out from behind Cloud and holds sun in air.

"Now that we have the sun and a few clouds, we need a lighthouse to protect the ships from any rocks that might be near the shore. And here's our lighthouse." Lighthouse-clown enters and takes position downstage center. Lighthouse-clown rotates, opening his mouth each time he faces the audience. This indicates the light.

"A slight breeze begins to blow across the waters." Breeze-clown enters side of stage blowing to create breeze.

"The blowing breeze causes the waters to have slight waves." Wave-clown enters and goes forward and back several times, making wave-like motions with his hands. As the Wave-clown goes across the stage for the third time, he puts on a white cap (whitecaps) and does one more pass.

"And a seagull circles the lighthouse, and returns out to sea." Seagull-clown enters stage, circles the Lighthouse, and leaves.

"And every beach must have it's bathing beauty." Bathing Beauty-clown enters, sets up a picnic on the beach and lies down to soak up the sun.

"The waters beckon to boaters. Even ones with oars." Boat-clown enters, sitting and rowing across the stage, but being careful not to boat on to the beach area.

"The fisherman comes down to the waters edge to try to catch the very elusive fish." Fisherman-clown enters with pole, and pretends to cast into the water. Fish-clown enters from other side of the stage, pretends to get hooked, but finally gets loose and swims away.

"But as evening sets in, the waters recede and the tide

comes in." Nothing happens. "I said, in the evening, the tide comes in." Nothing happens. Speaking louder, the storyteller continues, "I said, in the evening the TIDE comes in!" A clown enters from the side, carrying a huge box of Tide laundry detergent.

"No, not that kind of tide. Get out of here!" All clowns exit from stage with Storyteller chasing them.

The End

Note: Be creative with your costuming and performing. This can be a fun skit. You can add or subtract characters as you desire. Have fun with it.

TWELVE DAYS OF CLOWNING

Number of Clowns: Seven to twelve

Characters: New Clown, Piano Player, Powder Clown, prop clowns

Costumes: New Clown wears "new clown" tee-shirt, others wear regular clown wardrobe

Props: Piano with door on back, large and giant powder puffs, 8-10 boxes and cans of simulated make-up, 10 large shoes, 15 clown noses, 20 striped socks, 20 wigs, 24 pairs of gloves, 28 hats, 16 linking rings, 36 juggling balls, 20 cups of water on tray

Stage: Piano on one side (near center) with chair for piano player. The piano needs to be hollow so a clown can hide inside. A life-size homemade replica of a piano will do.

The Performance ━━━━━━━━━━━━━━━━━

This skit is based on the song "The Twelve Days of Christmas." You can write your own words, or use the words presented here. After the words are written, it is important to have them recorded on a cassette tape for use in your presentation, for no one actually sings during the skit. The New Clown merely mimes the words as the tape is playing. The skit begins as the piano player enters the stage, followed by the New Clown (who will be the soloist). Piano player takes a seat at the piano, and the New Clown steps onto position in front of the stage, preparing to sing this ballad. As each day of clowning is mentioned, a prop clown brings that item from backstage to the New Clown.

It is important that each item reach the New Clown just as it is mentioned in the song. Not all items are brought out every time (see schedule on page 190). Determine beforehand what running pattern the prop-clowns will use to enter and exit the stage, since there may be confusion. Having a predetermined running pattern will avoid possible collisions.

Select a small-size clown to work inside the piano. This clown (Powder Clown), comes out of the piano every time the song says, ". . . and some make-up and a big powder puff." When he comes out, he carries a large powder puff, filled with powder, and hits the New Clown immediately after the word "puff." It is advisable to have a can of powder and a small flashlight inside of the piano so that the Powder Clown can see what he is doing. If an upright piano is used the Powder Clown can simply hide behind it rather than inside of it.

On the twelfth day, the Power Clown brings out the giant powder puff and hits the New Clown with that. After being hit with the giant puff, the New Clown drops his pants, and chases the powder Clown off the stage. Music concludes and Piano Player gets up and takes a bow, as if nothing had happened on the stage.

The End

> *Note:* Not all items are brought out every time. There is enough confusion, and plenty of props, so the audience will not notice that all props are not always being brought out. Because of the number of prop-clowns, this is the only feasible way to do it. On the last day, however, all props are brought out.

Suggested Lyrics for the Song

On the FIRST DAY of clowning, the boss clown gave to me, some make-up and a big powder puff.

On the SECOND DAY of clowning, the boss clown gave to me, two giant shoes, and some make-up and a big powder puff.

On the THIRD DAY of clowning, the boss clown gave to me, three fake noses, two giant shoes, etc.

On the FOURTH DAY of clowning, the boss clown gave to me, four striped socks, three fake noses, etc.

On the FIFTH DAY of clowning, the boss clown gave to me, five different wigs, four striped socks, etc.

On the SIXTH DAY of clowning, the boss clown gave to me, six pairs of gloves, five different wigs, etc.

On the SEVENTH DAY of clowning, the boss clown gave to me, seven funny hats, six pairs of gloves, etc.

On the EIGHTH DAY of clowning, the boss clown gave to me, eight linking rings, seven funny hats, etc.

On the NINTH DAY of clowning, the boss clown gave to me, nine juggling balls, eight linking rings, etc.

On the TENTH DAY of clowning, the boss clown gave to me, ten walk-arounds, nine juggling balls, etc.

On the ELEVENTH DAY of clowning, the boss clown gave to me, eleven circus balloons, ten walk-arounds, etc.

On the TWELFTH DAY of clowning, the boss clown gave to me, twelve cups of water, eleven circus balloons, etc.

The pattern for delivering the props to the New Clown on the stage is as described below. This is set up for four prop clowns (B, C, D, and E). Clown A is the Powder Clown.

Item	Days											
	1	2	3	4	5	6	7	8	9	10	11	12
Puff	A	A	A	A	A	A	A	A	A	A	A	A
Makeup	B											C
Shoes		D		B				C			B	B
Noses			C		D		E		B			D
Socks				E		E		E		E		E
Wigs					C		C				C	C
Gloves						B		B		B		B
Hats							D		C		D	B
Rings								D				E
Balls									D	D	D	D
W/A's										C		C
Balloons											B	B
Water												D

For information or purchase of a cassette tape of the music for this skit, contact Barry DeChant, 14209 Ingram, Livonia, MI 48154.

190